Between God and Us

Between God and Us

How Covenants Connect Us to Heaven

Talks from the 2015
BYU Women's Conference

DESERET
BOOK

SALT LAKE CITY, UTAH

Library of Congress Cataloging-in-Publication Data

Names: Women's Conference (2015 : Brigham Young University)
Title: Between God and us : how covenants connect us to heaven: talks from the
    2015 BYU Women's Conference.
Description: Salt Lake City, Utah : Deseret Book, [2016] | ?2016
Identifiers: LCCN 2015044478 (print) | LCCN 2015048936 (ebook) |
    ISBN 9781629721873 (hardbound : alk. paper) | ISBN 9781629734187 (ebook)
Subjects: LCSH: Covenants—Religious aspects—Mormon Church—Congresses. |
    Mormon women—Religious life—Congresses.
Classification: LCC BX8657 .W66 2015 (print) | LCC BX8657 (ebook) |
    DDC 289.3/32082—dc23
LC record available at http://lccn.loc.gov/2015044478

Printed in the United States of America
Edwards Brothers Malloy, Ann Arbor, MI

10   9   8   7   6   5   4   3   2   1

Contents

Contents

Delighting in Our Covenants

Wendy Watson Nelson

When we really think about it, our covenants are a gift! A gift from God designed to get us safely back Home to Him![1]

What a gift that is![2]

My dear sisters, despite any anguishing life situation we may be in, it can feel like Christmas every day—if we truly receive the gift of our covenants every day! Clearly, Nephi had deep, joy-filled feelings about the gift of our covenants. His words are the theme for this year's conference: "My soul delighteth in the covenants of the Lord" (2 Nephi 11:5).

My sisters, I pray that the Holy Ghost will be the True Teacher as we consider the gift of our covenants with the Lord. We often refer to ourselves as "women of covenant" or as "covenant women." But what does that really mean? I've asked myself that question over and over again in recent months. I've also asked other women what it means to them.

One friend expressed it this way: "It means I've promised God that I will follow His Son—in what I do, think, and say. And I've made those promises by entering into sacred covenants

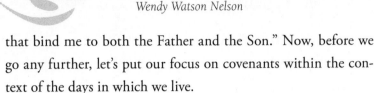

that bind me to both the Father and the Son." Now, before we go any further, let's put our focus on covenants within the context of the days in which we live.

People often ask my husband and me: "What's one of your favorite places you've ever visited?"

We typically answer—in unison, "Our backyard! A place we don't get to visit as often as we'd like!"

But seriously, one of my favorite places is Moscow, Russia! Why?

Because of what I experienced there within one twenty-four-hour period of time that commenced on Saturday, June 15, 2013.

While my husband taught the priesthood leaders of the area, I had the privilege of being with some of the sisters. I love our Russian sisters. They are spectacular!

That Saturday happened to be one of those rare spring planting days in Russia, so fewer than 100 of us were gathered.

When I stepped to the pulpit, I found myself saying something I'd never anticipated: "I'd like to get to know you by lineage. Please stand as the name of the tribe of Israel, as declared in your patriarchal blessing, is spoken." These women knew each other, but they didn't know each other's lineage.

As the names of the twelve tribes of Israel were announced—from Asher to Zebulon—and as the women stood, we were all amazed with what we were witnessing, feeling, and being taught.

We were being taught about the reality of the days in which we now live!

How many of the twelve tribes of Israel do you think were represented in that small gathering of fewer than 100 women—on that Saturday in Moscow?

Eleven! Eleven of the twelve tribes!

All but the tribe of Levi!

Now, here's another question: How fast does news travel where you live? Pretty fast? Well, it certainly travels quickly in Eastern Europe! I went directly from that unforgettable gathering to the airport to meet my husband. We then flew to Yerevan, Armenia, where he was to create the first stake of Zion in that country the next day.

The first people we met as we got off the plane in Armenia were the mission president and his wife. The first thing she said to me was, "I've got Levi!"

Just imagine: One of their missionaries—from Gilbert, Arizona, no less—was of the tribe of Levi!

When I was a little girl attending Primary in Raymond, Alberta, Canada, I was taught that in the last days before the Second Coming of the Savior, the twelve tribes would be gathered. That was always thrilling, and a little overwhelming, to think about!

So, imagine what it was like for me to *be with* children from *all* twelve tribes of Israel within one twenty-four-hour period of time!

It was far beyond thrilling. And very overwhelming!

My dear sisters, these are the latter days!

There has *never* been a time like this in the history of this earth. Ever!

There has never been a more important time than right now to understand the gift our Father has given us as He allows us to make covenants with Him.

One young mother expressed our privilege so well. She said:

"To be able to make a covenant with God makes me feel as though I matter. I really do have a purpose in the great plan of it all. There is no third party or agent 'signing' on my behalf or the Lord's. The promise, the covenant, I make is directly with the Lord!"

Sisters, there has never been a more important time to understand the power to which we have access because of our covenants than right now! And when we understand the *gift* of our covenants—and the power of God that flows to us through them—we, like Nephi, will truly delight in the covenants of the Lord![3]

For the past several months, I've been thinking nonstop about covenants. I've immersed myself in the scriptures; studied the words of prophets, seers, and revelators; and listened more attentively than ever to the words of our baptismal, sacramental, and temple covenants.

I've asked great women from various places around the world—from Preston, England, to Tokyo, Japan—what it means to them that they have made covenants with God.

Further, as I have immersed myself in family history research, I've felt the unmistakable urgency of those living on the other side of the veil who are desperate to make covenants with God—*now!*

After all that, I've come to the following conclusion: When it comes to making and keeping covenants with God, nothing is more important! And nothing is more filled with power!

I'll never forget a fascinating interchange I had with a young friend I'll call Amy. Late one Saturday evening, when my husband was out of town on assignment, I was working against the clock to complete a major project. I received an e-mail from Amy, who was in distress.

She wrote: "I was asked to speak, last minute, at my ward Relief Society activity this Wednesday. The topic is stress. I sent out a survey last night to seventy-five of the women here in BYU married student housing to find out what is stressing them out. After receiving their responses, I realize that I NEED HELP!"

As I read through the survey responses that Amy forwarded to me, these young wives and mothers reported they were experiencing stress, depression, anxiety, and marital intimacy problems. They listed as the cause of their problems: school, finances, lack of sleep, housework, homework, feelings of failing at everything, and an inability to balance all of their responsibilities.

I wondered how I should respond to Amy. What would really make a difference for these women? And what could be offered, during a twenty-two-minute Relief Society message, that could *possibly* reduce the real-life distress of these young mothers?

As I thought about Amy's difficult assignment, my experiences with family history and temple work filled my mind.

As counterintuitive as this may seem, I felt strongly impressed, in a way I could not deny, to encourage Amy to offer a twenty-one-day experiment to her Relief Society sisters.

So, I e-mailed back: "Invite the sisters to make a sacrifice of time to the Lord—by increasing their time in family history work and in temple work for the next twenty-one days."

Amy accepted this suggestion, and the results were remarkable!

Here are just three examples of what happened.

One young wife and mother wrote: "During the twenty-one

days that I increased my temple attendance and my family history work, I not only felt happier, I felt a sense of relief. I felt a weight had been taken off my chest.

When I made time to do these things—which is hard because we all are busy—I found that somehow I had more time to get other things done that needed to be done."

Another woman experienced a significant decrease in anxiety that had previously required medication. Her positive changes in mood, energy, and inspiration were so dramatic that she wrote: "My husband started to pray in gratitude for the increased Spirit in our home, which has occurred since I have been making sacrifices of time to the Lord in temple and family history work."

And yet another sister reported: "I have a two year old, and just had a baby last week.

"The twenty-one-day experiment helped with the end of my pregnancy.

"The sacrifice of time to do family history was something I could do sitting down, that was productive, and brought the Spirit!

"It gave me more purpose and helped me not to focus on the discomforts of the end of my pregnancy."

Sisters, my suggestion to a group of overtaxed, exhausted young mothers might seem not only counterintuitive but almost cruel. And with results that seem highly improbable! Why would I ask a woman who feels as though she's barely surviving to make a sacrifice of time to the Lord?

But these young mothers proved that sacrifice works. It works for women who have made covenants with God. Why?

Because when covenant women keep their covenants, they have greater access to the power of God!

The power of God flows into them, and that power, His power, generates a decrease in stress, an increase in energy, more and clearer revelation for their lives, renewed focus, courage to make needed changes, an increase in patience, and more time for what matters!

That's what these young mothers taught me as they kept their covenant of sacrifice!

Elder D. Todd Christofferson taught that increased spiritual power comes to us as we keep our covenants. He was explicit in his counsel that "in times of distress, let your covenants be paramount and let your obedience be exact."[4] That's *exactly* what those young covenant women did!

They were in distress, they focused on their covenant of sacrifice—they let that covenant be paramount—and their "obedience [was] exact."

And what happened?

Their distress fell away!

Would you be willing to try an experiment?

What would happen if, within the next six months, you selected a twenty-one-day period of time and then did *whatever* it took to make a sacrifice of time to the Lord by increasing the time you spend in doing family history and temple work during those twenty-one days? What blessings, miracles, and other positive changes would come to your life?

Sisters, just as keeping our covenant of sacrifice will bring the power of God to our lives, I've learned from covenant women

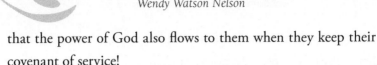

that the power of God also flows to them when they keep their covenant of service!

While the world would tell women that the very best way to be rejuvenated is by taking a vacation, or going on a shopping spree, or visiting a spa, I believe that *covenant* women are far more likely to be rejuvenated through serving, especially if they are able to delight in that covenant with others. I learned that principle some years ago at BYU Women's Conference. I was serving then as the women's conference chair. During our months of planning, several of us had the idea that adding a service project to the conference would be powerful.

The idea felt inspired.

We thought others would cheer, but we were wrong.

Dead wrong.

Some on the committee felt strongly that a service project would backfire. One statement made during an energetic discussion is emblazoned upon my memory: "Women don't come to Women's Conference to serve, they come to relax and get away from it all!"

Gratefully, the Relief Society General Presidency saw wisdom in the idea, and ultimately the very first service event at a BYU Women's Conference unfolded.

That pioneering effort was thrilling!

It was successful beyond anything any of us imagined, even though the outcome now pales in comparison to the service rendered at this conference now every year.

I am even more convinced now, years later, that weary covenant women are *revitalized* as the power of God flows into their lives when they keep their covenant of service.

As we keep our covenants, to what else do we have access? The Prophet Joseph Smith declared that if we, as covenant women, "live up to [our] *privilege*," the angels cannot be restrained from being our associates.[5]

Our "privilege" includes our covenants.

Our covenants are a privilege.

Therefore, as we live up to our *covenants*, the angels will not be able to be restrained from being our associates.

We could also say it this way: As we keep our covenants, we can ask for angels to help us. Literally!

It was during Elder Jeffrey R. Holland's April 2010 general conference talk that I first learned this truth. He said, "Ask for angels to help you."[6]

He said it with such clarity, and yet he said it in a manner that implied this was something we all knew!

But for me it was an entirely new principle.

I wanted to call out, "Wait! Wait! What? You mean I could have been asking for angels to help me all this time?"

Without intending to sound too dramatic, I can say with all candor that Elder Holland's six words changed my life:

"Ask for angels to help you."

That counsel changed my prayers.

It changed my understanding of the very real help from heaven that is always available to us *as we keep our covenants.*

I started to ask for assistance from those on the other side of the veil from that moment on!

Now, I'm not talking about praying for fantasy angels with wings to magically fairy-dust our problems away.

I'm not talking about praying *to* angels.

I'm talking about praying to our Heavenly Father, in the name of Jesus Christ, for those on the other side to be "dispatched"[7] (Elder Holland's word) to assist you.

Perhaps a departed loved one could be sent to help you with whatever you need.

Can you imagine the effort it took those angels who pushed from the rear of handcarts as they helped the pioneers over the steep, snowy, windy, freezing, jagged terrain of Rocky Ridge?

If angels can manage *that,* they can certainly help you and me over our present-day Rocky Ridges!

We know the Lord gets His work done with the help of His angels! So, could you use a little more help in your life?

If so, keep your covenants with more exactness than you ever have before!

And then ask for angels to help you with *whatever* you need.

Or ask for them to be dispatched to help those you love!

Does your child need help?

Is your husband in trouble?

Does your aunt need comfort?

Does your best friend need direction?

Ask for angels to be assigned to help them!

As a covenant-keeping woman, you can do that!

One of my former institute students, whom I'll call Barbara, followed through with that suggestion with thrilling results.

Barbara has served as proxy for many of my ancestors.

During a few temple sessions, Barbara had special experiences with a woman named Genevieve and with Genevieve's biological sisters. Barbara felt a deep connection with them.

So, she prayed and asked if Genevieve and her sisters, all of whom now live on the other side of the veil, could be dispatched to help Barbara's own sister, who lives on *this* side of the veil.

Barbara's sister had not been active in the Church for years, and she was having heart-wrenching difficulties with some rigorous life events.

Here are Barbara's words:

"I prayed that my sister could find peace in this world, that she could find direction back to Heavenly Father, and that the sisters of Genevieve could help her find her way back, and watch over her in this process.

A few weeks later my sister told me that she was taking her three boys to Church! Later she asked me how to get her patriarchal blessing. The eldest boy turned eight this summer and was baptized. And my sister is now attending temple preparation classes."

How can we explain such miracles?

Moroni tells us: "My beloved [sisters], have miracles ceased? Behold I say unto you, Nay; neither have angels ceased to minister unto the children of men. . . . And the office of their ministry is to call men [and women] unto repentance, and to fulfil and to do the work of the covenants of the Father" (Moroni 7:29–31).

Now, let's consider the power of perspective that our covenants can provide.

We know that our covenants with God did not start here on this earth, and they will not end here.

We know that we made covenants with God premortally.[8] Perhaps that's one of the reasons we "shouted for joy"! (see Job 38:7). Sisters, we are grateful for the veil of forgetfulness. It heightens the testing feature of our mortal probation.

And wow! What a test this is turning out to be—for each one of us!

But if the veil were lifted and we could look back, we would see ourselves as His spirit daughters making premortal covenants with God, our Heavenly Father.

Elder Neal A. Maxwell taught that we made premortal covenants about particular assignments, callings, and missions we would fulfill here on earth.[9] Perhaps that's why some callings bring such a reassuring feeling—at the very same time we feel so ill-prepared!

Fulfilling the wonderful missions for which we were sent to earth is one of the sure ways we can find peace and joy as we journey through this "spook alley" of mortal life.[10]

Elder John A. Widtsoe taught that we covenanted premortally to be partners with the Father and the Son in Their work to "bring to pass the immortality and eternal life of man" (Moses 1:39).[11] When we made that spectacular premortal covenant, did we ever imagine just how much time we would need to spend shepherding and rescuing others or how many hours studying and teaching and preaching the gospel?

Did we have *any clue* about the number of hours we would need to spend on the FamilySearch website? And the numerous hours in the temple that we would need to devote so we could fulfill *just that one* stunning premortal covenant?

Did we have any idea about how many activities we would need to *give up doing* so we would have time to help others return Home—to receive all that the Father hath? (see Luke 12:44).

My dear sisters, here is what I strongly believe: If we could see ourselves making our premortal covenants with our

Heavenly Father, *any and all* of our anguish, grief, and heartache would fall away. And we would say "Oh, now I remember! This heart-wrenching situation makes sense now!"[12]

That's the power of perspective our covenants can provide!

Now, consider this truth:

Commencing with Adam and Eve, *all* righteous men and women who love the Lord and have accepted His gospel have made covenants with Him!

Think of *any* of the covenant women down through the ages whom we love and admire—from Sarah and Rebekah to Sariah and Rachel; from Lois and Abish to Sister Noah and Sister Daniel; from Sister Peter to Sister James and Sister John; from Eve to Emma and Eliza.

Each of these women made *the very same covenants* with God that you and I made![13] Therefore, our covenants with God connect us with other women who have made covenants with God.

I love to think of that!

The very fact that temple covenants and ordinances seem *so different* from experiences during our Sunday worship meetings is yet another testimony of their truthfulness. They are ancient!

"The ancient of days"—meaning Adam, with Eve—received those covenants, our very covenants, from God![14]

Now, just for a moment, imagine two gigantic mirrors placed with their reflecting surfaces facing each other. Picture you and me with a Marriott Center-full of faithful—not perfect but faithful—Latter-day Saint women who are striving to keep their covenants[15] standing in front of one of the mirrors and looking into it with the other mirror parallel behind us.

What would we see? We would see numberless images of women stretching into infinity.

Can you picture that in your mind's eye?

Freeze-frame that image.

As you look at that image, you are seeing the number of covenant women with whom you and I are connected *each and every time* we make a covenant with God!

And each and every time we keep those sacred obligations!

It has been said that the present fascination some women have with social media is the need women have to be connected with other women!

To support each other, to know what's happening in each other's lives, to have other women know and approve of what we're doing.

We want "witnesses" for our lives!

With the image of the two parallel mirrors in mind, let's consider this question:

Do we, as covenant women, need more friends on Facebook, or do we need to experience more of the beautifully familiar, unmistakably divine feelings of being connected with—perhaps more accurately, reconnected with—*millions* of other women who have made covenants with God?

On a day when we don't think *anyone* cares about us and our struggles or all we've been trying to do, what would happen if we took just a moment to look, with our mind's eye, into those double mirrors and see the truth?

Because the truth is that *each and every day* you and I *let* our covenants influence our thoughts and words and actions, we are inseparably connected to millions and millions of covenant women. Women from the beginning of time down through each and every gospel dispensation!

Now, those are friends we hope will "like" us!

And now, to talk about another perspective, let me tell you of an unexpected journey I've been on for the past two and a half years. After studying repeatedly Elder Richard G. Scott's October 2012 general conference address, entitled "The Joy of Redeeming the Dead,"[16] I have changed from a woman who basically went into a coma whenever she heard the words "family history" to one who now feels an irrepressible urgency to find a birth, marriage, death or census record to uniquely identify one more ancestor! I am now a woman *desperately* driven by the desire not to waste time that I could have spent helping those who are *desperate* for covenants. And now, for me, super-sleuthing a mother's maiden name trumps watching any detective movie I used to enjoy. And no one is more surprised than I am! How did this happen?

When Elder Scott said to me, with fifteen million others listening in, "This work is a spiritual work,"[17] I believed him. And I found myself praying, "Please lead me to those who are ready to make covenants with Thee and receive their ordinances." That prayer opened the heavens for me.

When Elder Scott taught that "some sacrifice"[18] would be involved, I believed him. But what could I possibly sacrifice? I thought I was using my time *really* well on things that *really* mattered. Then I remembered the time I spent playing Scrabble by myself on my iPad. I didn't think that little bit of time could make any difference, but I set Scrabble aside for two months.

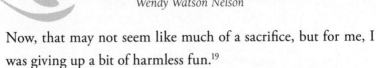

Now, that may not seem like much of a sacrifice, but for me, I was giving up a bit of harmless fun.[19]

Within the first two weeks of trying this new approach to family history, I learned three things I can never forget:

1. Those on the other side of the veil are very much alive—and perhaps not all that cheerful about being called "dead."

2. Those on the other side are eager—no, actually they are desperate—to receive their saving and exalting ordinances.

Covenants, and *only* covenants with their associated ordinances, have the power to unlock the gates behind which our ancestors live. So, as wonderful as it is to know stories about Grandma—for example, that she loved peaches and poems—if we don't do *whatever it takes* to ensure that she has the privilege to make covenants with God and receive her essential ordinances—guess what? Grandma is still in prison!

And I'm not sure just how long she's going to be cheerful about that!

3. The third thing I learned is that we are *the* only church on the planet with the power and authority from God to perform these ordinances.

Actually, I learned one other thing: Family history is really fun! Even more fun than Scrabble!

So, if you'd like a little more joy in your life, a little more meaning, more heart-to-heart connections, more focus, energy, motivation, more of so many wonderful things, *make time* to help those on the other side *make covenants* with God!

As you do so, the power of God will flow into your life in an unprecedented way.

What else can we do to keep and increase the flow of God's

power in our lives? President Gordon B. Hinckley taught a great truth at the dedication of the Conference Center in October 2000. In the concluding session of that general conference, President Hinckley's parting words included this counsel:

"The great 'Hosanna' salutation in which we participated this morning should remain an unforgettable experience. From time to time, we can repeat quietly in our minds, when we are alone, those beautiful words of worship."[20]

My dear sisters, if it is good for us to repeat quietly in our minds, when we are alone, the beautiful words of worship of the Hosanna salutation, wouldn't it be good for us to follow the same pattern with other beautiful words of worship?

What about the beautiful words of our baptismal and temple covenants and other sublime words spoken in the temple?

There is spiritual power in the words of our covenants.

Do we know the words?

Do we know what we said we would do?

Do we know what the Lord has promised?

Sometimes when we hear words frequently, they can become background noise rather than a foreground focus to help us worship.

But we can change that!

We can make a personal plan for learning and remembering the words of our covenants.

It will take some effort. But we can do it!

How would our experience with the sacrament change if we imagined the Savior to be the one blessing the bread and water just as He did for His Twelve Apostles?

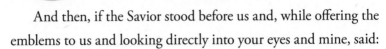

And then, if the Savior stood before us and, while offering the emblems to us and looking directly into your eyes and mine, said:

"Are you willing to take upon you *my* name this week?

"Are you willing to always remember *me*?

"Are you willing to keep *my* commandments this week?"

Would we then truly, and finally, experience a cleansing of our spirits[21] and "the wounds of [our spirits] being healed, and [our] load being lifted"?[22]

And what about our temple covenants?

What can change for us as we learn, feel deeply, and remember the words of our temple covenants?

Let me tell you about another young friend. Let's call her Jean. Jean was put on bed rest during her second pregnancy and couldn't attend the temple for a little while.

She wrote: "I was sincerely struggling with feelings of being pulled so many different ways and of entering a new season of life that just didn't lend itself to weekly temple attendance at that point.

"It was in response to these feelings and prayerful pleadings that the words entered my mind, 'You may not always be able to go through the temple, but you are always able to have the temple go through you.'

"That was my answer and the one I so desperately needed!"

Jean continued, "Now I daily repeat the words we say in the temple (in my mind, of course) every morning as I get ready for the day.

"I reverently and with power say those words in my mind.

"I recovenant and rededicate myself each new day."

Now, clearly, Jean had been paying close attention during her previous weekly time in the temple.

For many of us, we can start now.

Each time we go to the temple, we can really focus on and learn the words of one more covenant or perhaps those of one more associated ordinance.

And then we can do what President Hinckley advised: "From time to time, we can repeat quietly in our minds, when we are alone, those beautiful words of worship."[23]

A dear friend recently did just that on a day when she didn't feel well and yet was less than an hour away from needing to fulfill a major and highly stressful assignment.

She wrote, "As I waited alone in my car before the event and because I physically didn't feel well, I chose to focus on the words of the initiatory ordinance.

"As those words went through my mind, I actually started to feel a little bit better. Plus, they gave me a feeling of peace and assurance that somehow I'd get through the assignment." And she did.

Just think of the power that is available to us through sacred words of worship!

My husband taught this profound truth: "The greatest compliment that can be earned here in this life is to be known as a covenant keeper."[24]

My dear sisters, as we are covenant keepers, our covenants change everything in our lives—for the better!

They change our identity and our ultimate destination.

They change the road we're traveling on through this life, because now we're on the covenant path that leads back Home.[25]

And no worldly GPS can ever find that road!

As covenant keepers, what we want out of life; what we are willing to spend our time, energy, and money on; what we think is entertaining; what we think is appealing—all change.

As covenant keepers, our desire to be someone the Lord can count on increases exponentially. *No matter what* He asks us to do!

As covenant keepers, how we feel about the Savior changes forever!

He is real to us in a way He's never been before.

How we feel about His Atonement—changes.

We relish repentance.[26]

And we seek gifts of the Spirit—one by one—to turn our weak things into strengths! (See Ether 12:27.)

As covenant keepers, we find that our prayers change—because we are now bound to Heavenly Father, and we're tied closer than ever before to our Savior Jesus Christ![27]

Personal revelation becomes something we prepare for and expect![28]

As covenant keepers, we find that our past, present, and future can all change!

Everything can change for the better—as we keep our covenants.

Including our very nature![29] So, in the words of Elder Jeffrey R. Holland: "If you have made covenants, keep them.

"If you haven't made them, make them.

"If you have made them and broken them, repent and repair them."[30]

My dear covenant sisters, these latter-days are *our days!*

Are we ready?

We can be—as we make and keep our covenants with God.

We can be *morally strong* covenant women who are sin-resistant Saints (see 3 Nephi 20:25–26). Women who, because of time spent in the temple, know how to deal with the adversary and how to pray with power!

We can be *diligent* covenant-keeping women who are true disciples of Jesus Christ in this digital age and who know how to use technology—righteously![31]

We can be *articulate* covenant-keeping women who are consistently seeking to understand the doctrine of Jesus Christ, so we are not swayed by "every wind of doctrine" (Ephesians 4:14) that blows through a blog!

We can be *wise* covenant-keeping women who eagerly remove from our lives *anything* that is preventing us from receiving even more of God's power.

We can be *enlightened* covenant-keeping women who seek to understand more about our covenants. Women who know that when we let the Lord know that we are serious about learning more, *He* will teach us!

It is my testimony, my dear sisters, that there is *nothing* more important than making covenants with God and then keeping them with increasing precision. Making covenants with God calls forth the divine within us. And keeping our covenants with God allows Him to pour His divine power into us.

An Exchange of Love between God and Us

Bonnie L. Oscarson

It is a joy to discuss covenants as an exchange of love between us and our Heavenly Father because I have a strong and firm testimony that it is true. If my three years serving as a temple matron in the Stockholm Sweden Temple taught me anything at all, it is that our Father loves His children, we are central to His work, He is aware of the intimate details of our lives, and He stands ever ready and anxious to bless us with every possible good thing He can. This is especially true as we make every effort possible to honor our covenants with Him. In return, we show our love for our Heavenly Father by our willingness to enter into a covenant relationship with Him and the manner in which we choose to live up to those covenants.

A STORY OF PROMISES THAT WERE A BLESSING

An example from the life of my daughter Emily illustrates how covenants are an evidence of the love which both generates the need for a promise and is the motivation for keeping a promise. We were living in Houston, Texas, when Emily attended

Brigham Young University in Provo, Utah. While she was home with us for a short break one summer, she went on a date with a young man from our ward with whom she had attended church, seminary, and school since she was fifteen years old. He was on a football scholarship at the United States Naval Academy and also home for a short time. Even though they had been friends for five years, something clicked that summer and they saw each other every day during the time they were home. Both felt that a relationship was something worth exploring. They continued their relationship long-distance between Annapolis, Maryland, and Provo, Utah, for the next year and they both stopped dating other people. About one year into their relationship, Emily flew to the east coast for a big dance and Clark proposed to her on the top of the Empire State Building. It was like a story from a movie. Midshipmen from the Naval Academy are not permitted to get married until after they graduate. Emily graduated in December, but Clark had another semester to go. Emily approached us, as her parents, with the idea that she wanted to move to Maryland to work while Clark finished school so she could be near him.

We understood her desire to be close to the man of her dreams, especially since they had not been able to spend a lot of time together during their courtship. She found an apartment to share with some other young women who were also engaged to midshipmen and planned to sign up with a temp agency to help her find a job. Her father and I had a few concerns. We trusted our daughter and knew that she had always planned to marry in the temple, but we saw some dangers in a situation where her fiancé would have his weekends free and as a senior didn't have to stay on campus.

Out of our love and concern for Emily, we told her that we would give our blessing to her plan if she would promise us one thing—that Clark would never spend the night at her apartment, even if the others she was living with did not follow the same rule. Out of Emily's love and respect for our concern as her parents, her love of the Lord, and because she also understood the risks and temptations, she agreed to the promise and so did Clark.

Emily's bishop saw wisdom in her going to the temple and receiving her endowments at the beginning of her move to Annapolis and it turned out to be a wonderful blessing to her and her fiancé. She and Clark attended the Washington DC Temple every weekend together as they made plans for their marriage. The covenants they had both made when they received their endowments were a strength and reminder to them of their goals and the standards they needed to keep in order to reach them. They kept their promise that he would never spend the night at her apartment.

On June 1, 2000, just a week and a day after Clark's graduation from the Naval Academy, they were married in the Dallas Texas Temple and they are now the parents of four girls, one boy, and are expecting a sixth child in November. Clark is currently serving as the bishop of their ward in Houston. Emily has since told me that us asking them to make that promise was the best thing we could have done and was a great blessing to them in their courtship.

Isn't this similar to what our Heavenly Father does for us? He sees the dangers of this earthly life and understands the possible risks to our happiness and salvation much better than we do. He has an eternal perspective. He is anxious for us to be happy and knows our best chance for that is obedience to His commandments. He asks us to promise Him certain things that will help prepare us to return to Him someday. In return, even though we may not always understand the reasons, because we love and trust our Father we are willing to do as He asks.

God's Love Is Certain and Assured

Can we, as limited mortals, begin to comprehend the depth and magnitude of the love which God feels for His children? One of the most tender and poignant scriptural descriptions of God's love is found in the account of Enoch's profound vision and personal conversation with the Lord found in Moses 7. As God looks upon those who choose to reject Him, Enoch is surprised to see God weep. Enoch asks, "How is it that thou canst weep, seeing thou art holy, and from all eternity to all eternity?" (v. 29). The Lord replies, "Behold these thy brethren; they are the workmanship of mine own hands, . . . I created them" (v. 32). The Lord then describes their hatred for one another and the inevitable result: "Misery shall be their doom; . . . wherefore should not the heavens weep, seeing these shall suffer?" (v. 37). These moving passages give an insight into the tender feelings of a parent who also happens to be divine and eternal. He yearns for the happiness of His children—and even God Himself feels sorrow when we choose wickedness.

In the Book of Mormon we find other evidences of God's love for His children. Lehi sees in vision a tree "whose fruit was desirable to make one happy" (1 Nephi 8:10) and which when he ate "filled my soul with exceedingly great joy," which makes "it . . . desirable above all other fruit" (1 Nephi 8:12). When

Nephi is shown his father's vision, it is interesting that the scenes which Lehi saw are shown to Nephi in the context of the life and ministry of the Savior, Jesus Christ. Nephi is taught that the tree represents the "love of God, which sheddeth itself abroad in the hearts of the children of men; wherefore, it is the most desirable above all things. . . . and the most joyous to the soul" (1 Nephi 11:22, 23). He is then immediately shown "the Son of God going forth among the children of men" (1 Nephi 11:24). The lesson for me is that Jesus Christ, the Son of God, is the literal embodiment of God's love for His children.

John teaches, "For God so loved the world, that he gave his only begotten Son, that whosoever believeth in him should not perish, but have everlasting life" (John 3:16). Elder D. Todd Christofferson has said that this verse in John embodies the "new and everlasting covenant in one sentence."[1]

COVENANTS ARE EVIDENCE OF GOD'S LOVE FOR HIS CHILDREN

This brings us to the role which covenants play in connection with God's love for His children. Covenants are agreements between God and man where God sets the terms. Elder Christofferson explains, "In these divine agreements, God binds Himself to sustain, sanctify, and exalt us in return for our commitment to serve Him and keep His commandments."[2] God asks us to enter into these binding agreements, these covenants with Him, because He loves us and He knows that binding us to Him—essentially making God our partner in this life—is the only possible way that we have a hope of returning to Him and receiving exaltation in His kingdom. "For behold, this is my work and my glory—to bring to pass the immortality and eternal life of man" (Moses 1:39). He accomplishes this work through covenants. Think of it! God invites us to come out of our worldly sphere and to enter His sphere through covenants. We are invited to join Him, to partner with Him in our salvation and in the salvation of all of His children.

The covenants God offers us begin when we are still children. He understands the importance of setting us on the covenant path as soon as we are ready to understand the importance and value of keeping the commandments. When we are baptized, we enter into a covenant relationship with God. We become His covenant children. As early as age eight, we show we are willing to enter His kingdom and keep His commandments from that day forward. We learn from the Book of Mormon that we also promise "to stand as witnesses of God at all times and in all things, and in all places that ye may be in, even until death" (Mosiah 18:9). Elder Neal A. Maxwell called it taking on the "duties of disciple-ship"[3] and the Lord invites us to begin even when we are children.

It is no small thing that this is the only ordinance that, with its associated covenant, we are invited to participate in and renew every single week for the rest of our lives through the ordinance of the sacrament. Because Heavenly Father loves us, He provides a way for us to remember, renew, and recommit to the covenants we make at baptism—weekly. It is that important. Few have taught this principle more beautifully than Elder Jeffrey R. Holland, who said this about the ordinance of the sacrament: "Since that upper room experience on the eve of Gethsemane and Golgotha, children of the promise have been under covenant to remember Christ's sacrifice in this newer, higher, more holy and personal

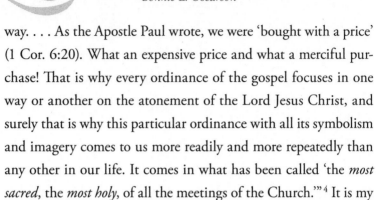
way. . . . As the Apostle Paul wrote, we were 'bought with a price' (1 Cor. 6:20). What an expensive price and what a merciful purchase! That is why every ordinance of the gospel focuses in one way or another on the atonement of the Lord Jesus Christ, and surely that is why this particular ordinance with all its symbolism and imagery comes to us more readily and more repeatedly than any other in our life. It comes in what has been called 'the *most sacred*, the *most holy*, of all the meetings of the Church.'"[4] It is my hope that we may all make more of an effort each week to see the love of our Father in that holy moment and make the partaking of the sacrament the most sacred part of our week.

TEMPLES ARE EVIDENCE OF GOD'S LOVE AND A PLACE FOR MAKING COVENANTS

Our temples are another of the great evidences of the love our Heavenly Father has for His children, because it is there that we make the most sacred and binding covenants with Him. The Lord has provided a sacred and hallowed place where His children can be taught from on high, sanctified, and endowed with power (see D&C 43:16). It was Elder Carlos E. Asay who said, "I regard the ordinances of the endowment as an exchange of love between God, Our Father, and us. We . . . know that the Only Begotten Son, even Jesus the Christ, 'so loved the world that he gave his own life, that as many as would believe might become the sons of God.' (D&C 34:3). Thus, every commandment, every ordinance, every covenant, every law, every 'thou shalt,' every 'thou shalt not,' and every teaching received from Our Father in Heaven and His Son, Our Savior—especially those received in the House of the Lord—is an expression of divine love."[5]

I have a sister-in-law who is now on the other side of the veil, whose name was also Bonnie L. Oscarson. Trust me when I say it was always confusing at family gatherings. She once told us a story about when she was a teenager growing up in St. Louis, Missouri. One of her best friends was named Grace; she was not a member of the Church. Grace's mother had passed away when she was small and she was being raised by her father. Once, Bonnie and Grace were both invited to attend a party that sounded like it was going to be a little on the wild side. They both went to their parents to ask if they could go and Grace was given permission. However, when Bonnie approached her parents, they must have been aware of the circumstances surrounding this party and they told Bonnie no—she couldn't go. When Bonnie reported this to her friend, Grace began to cry. Bonnie thought at first that she was disappointed that she couldn't go the party, but through her tears Grace made this remarkably insightful comment: "I wish that my father loved me enough to tell me no sometimes." She was wise beyond her years in recognizing that a kind and loving parent sets boundaries and gives guidelines to provide their child with safety, protection, and help to avoid those things which might bring harm. A loving parent takes the time to give a child instructions and tools for meeting the challenges of life. The temple is the place where we are able to receive loving instruction, help, and guidance from a concerned Father and every aspect of the temple is evidence of His love for His children.

For example, we are taught in the temple that when Adam and Eve were cast out of the Garden of Eden, they weren't sent into the world unprotected. It says in Moses 4:27, "Unto Adam, and also unto his wife, did I, the Lord God, make coats of skins, and clothed them." In the initiatory ordinances of the temple we also receive a garment and are taught of the promises associated with it, which to me are touching and beautiful evidence of our Father's love and concern for us as His children. In his book *The Holy Temple*, President Boyd K. Packer of the Quorum of the Twelve Apostles explained this about the temple garment: "The garment represents sacred covenants. It fosters modesty and becomes a shield and protection to the wearer."[6] The Father has also provided protection for us.

Elder Carlos E. Asay, a former president of the Salt Lake Temple, made this wonderful observation about the temple garment: "I like to think of the garment as the Lord's way of letting us take part of the temple with us when we leave. It is true that we carry from the Lord's house inspired teachings and sacred covenants written in our minds and hearts. However, the one tangible remembrance we carry with us back into the world is the garment. And though we cannot always be in the temple, a part of it can always be with us to bless our lives."[7]

Through the years as I have sought to understand the blessings and promises associated with the proper wearing of my temple garments, I have come to see myself as being wrapped in the love of my Heavenly Father and I treasure the comforting assurances which accompany the proper wearing of the garment.

Another way in which the temple and its associated covenants symbolize the love of our Heavenly Father is that the temple provides a way for all of His children to return to Him, including those people who lived on the earth before the gospel and essential priesthood ordinances were restored. Do you know of any other religion in the world which offers the saving ordinances of the gospel for those millions of people who lived and died on this earth without the possibility of receiving them? We are truly unique in this belief which teaches us how precious and dear each and every individual is to our Father, no matter when or where they lived on the earth.

Through researching the names of our ancestors and taking their names to the temple we become partners with God in providing saving ordinances for His children. The work is filled with miracles. If even a lowly sparrow cannot fall to the ground without our Heavenly Father knowing of it (see Matthew 10:29), how much more must He be concerned when a child is lost. Let me explain. My husband is an avid genealogist and has spent countless hours researching the names of his Swedish ancestors. I would like to share an experience which he wrote down and shared with our children in an e-mail while we were serving in the temple in Sweden.

"We were blessed with a special experience this past week. I've been tracking the ancestry of the husband of my dad's favorite aunt in Sweden, Aunt Mathilda. The temple work for the first few generations was completed in the Salt Lake Temple in the 1930s. But I was impressed to retrace some of the steps that someone had taken to find this information seventy or eighty years ago. Pehr Nilsson, born in 1782, and Brita Helena Larsdotter had been sealed to their six children. In digging through the records, however, I discovered a little girl, Anna Brita Pehrsdotter, who was born in 1816 but died in 1820 at the age of four. This little girl had been lost. Parents and siblings were sealed. The work was done. And for eighty years this little girl has been waiting for someone to find her and help her

become a part of this 'Forever Family.' Why did I choose this particular line to follow? How did I come across this information? I know it wasn't by accident. Friday evening, I had the opportunity to conduct a sealing session. I was moved to tears as I performed the ordinance that made Anna Brita a part of her family for eternity. I know she was aware of what was happening as well as her parents and her siblings. I thought especially of her older sister, Maja Stina, who was ten when her little sister passed away. It was no fluke that Anna Brita was found. The Lord knows her and kept His promise that someday she would be together with her family. The Lord keeps all His promises."[8]

What a joyous work it is to be a partner with the Lord in seeking out, identifying, and performing saving ordinances for God's children whose names have not been spoken aloud for perhaps hundreds of years and who may fear that they have been forgotten. The Lord does not forget any of His children and the ordinances and covenants of the temple are for everyone—both the living and the dead. What love and mercy are evident in this work.

During our three years serving in the temple in Stockholm, the most significant and memorable moments for me were the sealings of husbands, wives, and families to each other. When young (and a few not-so-young) couples knelt across the altars in the temple from one another, I could sense the great significance of what was taking place each and every time. The Spirit was stronger on those occasions than at just about any other time in the temple.

When my husband officiated as the sealer, he would often remind these couples that there were many people both seen and unseen who were aware of, and rejoicing for, what they were about to do—make sacred covenants with each other and with God that would be the beginning of an eternal family. The event has eternal implications for both those who have gone before— their ancestors—and their future posterity. There must be rejoicing on both sides of the veil each time a couple is sealed in the temple. What a great gift from a loving Father in Heaven. Is there any greater evidence of His love for His children than that of the sealing power that promises that marriages and families can last through eternity?

Honoring Our Covenants Is Evidence of Our Love for Heavenly Father and His Son, Jesus Christ

I have spoken a lot about our Heavenly Father's love for us and the myriad ways He shows it through the covenants He has made available to us. I also want to discuss how we show our love for Heavenly Father and His Son, Jesus Christ, through how we keep our covenants. The title of this talk suggests that covenants are an exchange of love between God and us. How do we show *our* love of God through covenants?

John teaches the answer simply and clearly, "If ye love me, keep my commandments" (John 14:15). I also love this scrip-ture from the Doctrine and Covenants: "Be faithful and dili-gent in keeping the commandments of God, and I will encircle thee in the arms of my love" (D&C 6:20). It's simply beautiful and beautifully simple. We show our love for God by keeping His commandments and honoring our covenants. In return, He shows an increase of love for us.

Elder Donald L. Staheli quoted President Ezra Taft Benson

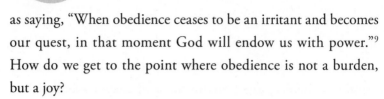

as saying, "When obedience ceases to be an irritant and becomes our quest, in that moment God will endow us with power."[9] How do we get to the point where obedience is not a burden, but a joy?

Loving the Lord is the answer. Love is the greatest and purest motivation I can think of for honoring our covenants. Elder Donald L. Hallstrom has observed, "Love is the most powerful motivator of all. We will make sacrifices and bear burdens for those we love that we would not endure for any other reason—not for money, not for recognition, not for power. If love does not exist, our commitment will surely wane."[10] If love is the best motivation for honoring our promises to the Lord, and if we show the Lord how much we love Him by keeping His commandments, how do we increase our love for the Lord?

The best answer for that comes from our experiences as women. Women are unusually good at sacrificing for others—our friends, our husbands, our parents, and especially our children. It is something that often comes more naturally to us as women, especially where our children are concerned. Do you ever find yourself asking why you love the little stinkers so much?

The answer can be found as you think about what motherhood can entail. It often begins with morning sickness, leg cramps, heartburn—and let's not even talk about the birthing process. Then there are the 2:00 A.M. feedings, 4:00 A.M. feedings, 6:00 A.M. feedings and all the cleaning-ups of the coming-outs—for at least two years—per child. Did I mention spit-up and clothing changes (yours and theirs), teething, or walking the floor with feverish little bodies wrapped in our arms? I may as well mention tantrums, car sickness, self-administered haircuts, permanent marker art on the wooden floor—and did you know that when you smear a tub of margarine all over the kitchen floor it is like an indoor ice rink for you and a younger sister? I do.

In the midst of all of this, and much, much more, have you noticed something else about being a mother? Every little act of service, every small sacrifice made, each and every effort made to care for, love, and protect a child, wraps another thread of love around your heart and soul until, before you know it, you and that child are bound together—not with threads, but with steel bands of incredible strength. You would go to any lengths, you would put yourself in harm's way, and you would even give your life for that child's happiness.

There is a psychological principle that says that we will love those most for whom we sacrifice the most. The bond between us and our children is so intense because we spend the first decade of their lives—and more—taking care of their every need. If we want to increase our love for our husbands, we find ways to serve them. If we want to increase our love for someone, whether it is an enemy or a friend, the answer is to serve them. The same is true when it concerns our relationship with the Lord. The more we serve Him through our service to others and in Church callings, the more love we have for Him. As our love for the Lord increases, our desire to please Him through our obedience increases. Conversely, as Elder Hallstrom said, "If love does not exist, our commitment will surely wane."[11]

Sometimes we can be rather subtle in the keeping of our covenants. We live the gospel haphazardly or do only the bare minimum. It is easy to become like the Jewish leaders in Christ's time who lived the letter of the law but were lacking the spirit of

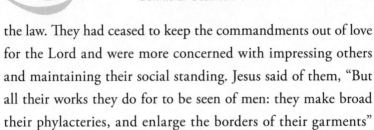

the law. They had ceased to keep the commandments out of love for the Lord and were more concerned with impressing others and maintaining their social standing. Jesus said of them, "But all their works they do for to be seen of men: they make broad their phylacteries, and enlarge the borders of their garments" (Matthew 23:5).

When we truly love the Lord, we will be generous in how we keep our covenants—willing to keep the commandments and take it one or two steps beyond. We won't just pay the exact amount for the cost of two meals for a fast offering; we will be generous and give much more. We won't just avoid shopping or sporting events on the Sabbath day; we will fill the day with service, good works, and personal and family enrichment. We won't just avoid coffee, tea, and tobacco because that is what is spelled out specifically in the Word of Wisdom, but we will exercise and get enough sleep and show how much we value and respect our bodies by the way we take care of them even in the way we dress. We will stand as witnesses of Christ even when no one is looking, because we love the Lord and delight to obey Him. "For this is the love of God, that we keep his commandments: and his commandments are not grievous" (1 John 5:3).

In the temple we make covenants to be obedient, to live a pure and chaste life, and "we covenant with the Lord to devote our time, talents, and means to His kingdom."[12] Temple covenants are not for those who are lukewarm about their testimonies. The Lord asks us to be completely committed to Him and to building His kingdom on earth by serving others.

I would like to share a story about a couple who had made temple covenants and who were generous in living them. When we were serving in the temple in Stockholm, one day a man named Brother Strandberg came to the temple. He was from a little town in southern Sweden called Kristianstad. When my husband heard the name of the town he told Brother Strandberg that the Kristianstad Branch held a very special place in his heart because of an experience we had while serving as mission president and wife in Sweden many years ago. Listen to my husband's own words:

"Shortly after the creation of the Sweden Göteborg Mission, we were faced with a difficult problem. The little branch in Kristianstad was really struggling. The lack of priesthood leadership in the branch had led us to consider dismantling the branch by combining it with the branch in Malmö (which is about sixty miles from Kristianstad). While this may have made sense organizationally, there was one thing that gnawed at us. There were a few youth in Kristianstad that would never be able to enjoy the full blessings of membership living that far away. As a presidency, we prayed and sought the Lord's help in knowing what we should do. A solution came to mind. If Brigham Young could call families to move from one place to another to build up the kingdom, why couldn't we? [This was at a time in the Church when there were few senior couples serving missions and we had none in Sweden at the time.] I called Elder Joseph B. Wirthlin, our Area Supervisor at the time in Frankfurt, and asked for permission. He supported the idea and we asked Brother Anders and Sister Margit Mårdby to come to the mission office.

"After many years working for the railroad, Brother Mårdby had just reached that point that all working people look forward to . . . retirement! At last, to be home and do the things he had

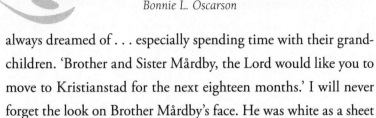

always dreamed of . . . especially spending time with their grand-children. 'Brother and Sister Mårdby, the Lord would like you to move to Kristianstad for the next eighteen months.' I will never forget the look on Brother Mårdby's face. He was white as a sheet . . . totally shocked. They asked for time to think about it.

"It didn't take long before they called and accepted. They moved to Kristianstad. Anders was called to be branch president and Margit president of the Relief Society. The Mårdbys (and the Nordlanders, who followed) literally saved the branch. They visited members, planned activities and taught the gospel."[13]

When my husband finished relating this story, Brother Strandberg replied with emotion, "I was one of those youth."

They both shed a tear as Brother Strandberg went on to say that of the six youth in the branch at the time the Mårdbys came, five of them still live in Kristianstad and five of the six are active members of the church. All six youth served missions. They served in England (two of them), Scotland, the Philippines, Denmark, and Norway. Three have been either a bishop or branch president, and one was currently the stake president of the Malmö Sweden Stake. One cannot help but wonder how many lives have been touched and blessed because the Mårdbys took their covenant of consecration seriously, even though at the time it was the last thing they wanted to do. This brother we met in the temple that day, his family, and perhaps thousands of others will be eternally grateful that Anders and Margit Mårdby loved the Lord and were willing to keep the covenants they had made in the temple. Sisters, we show our love for the Lord by generously keeping our covenants with Him in everything we do in our lives.

CONCLUSION

The prophet Nephi saw in vision the blessings promised to those who are righteous covenant keepers: "And it came to pass that I, Nephi, beheld the power of the Lamb of God, that it descended upon the saints of the church of the Lamb, and upon the covenant people of the Lord, who were scattered upon all the face of the earth; and they were armed with righteousness and with the power of God in great glory" (1 Nephi 14:14). What glorious promises are given to the Lord's covenant people—evidence of His love for us. No wonder we love and honor Him. The Apostle John said, "We love him, because he first loved us" (1 John 4:19).

I testify this day that our Heavenly Father and His Son, Jesus Christ, live and direct the work of this Church. They love us with a love that is beyond our ability to comprehend. The covenants they ask us to make and keep at baptism, when we partake of the sacrament, and in our sacred temples are evidence that they want to be intimately involved in our lives and they want to help us return to Their presence. Covenants bind us to our Heavenly Father. They make Him a partner in all that we do in this life. We know that God always keeps His promises and that He will never let us down. I testify that love of the Lord and gratitude for all that He has done for us are the greatest reasons for us to keep our covenants with Him. He gave His Only Begotten Son so that we might have hope for exaltation. May we commit to keep our covenants generously and with love.

The Light That Endures

Mary Kathleen Eyring

I would like to share some thoughts on the eternal value of things that don't keep. My brother and I recently spent a weekend cleaning out the basement of my parents' home of nearly forty years. Their basement, like most basements, is a repository for things they seldom use and care for either very much—or not at all. When we had separated the treasures from the dross, my brother and I began to pore over the things my mother has preserved over a half-century of marriage and motherhood. She is not a materialistic person, and so the scope and the depth of her archive surprised us. Her boxes hold photographs, picture frames, vases, greeting cards, the Christmas wish lists of her children, and countless books and church talks on parenting, education, and faith. Her cluttered basement is a detailed testament to her love of her parents, her husband, her children, and the Lord.

Many of us are similarly devoted to physical objects we invest with sentimental and even spiritual value. I have learned from examining the things my mother has kept and treasured that these objects can indeed have great value—not for what they do, but for what *we* do *with them*. It's a reality that even objects we love and care for don't last forever. For example, no matter how carefully we curate a photographic record of our lives, none of us can take that record with us to the next life or even reliably pass it on to posterity. And yet, every day, we invest our time and talent and energy and faith into a hundred things that don't keep. The food we make disappears or spoils; rain falls on the car we wash; the crises at work and home we put to bed breed a thicket of fresh challenges. When we look around and don't see evidence of it, we may well ask, "Have I done any good in the world today?" I think the answer is often *yes*, but the evidence is spiritual rather than physical. Even when the things we toil over are eaten, stained, spoiled, used up, worn out, or finally relegated to basement shelves, the light of our consecrated efforts continues to burn in the hearts of the people we love and serve.

The service we offer to those whom we love is a fulfillment of the covenant we make at baptism. The words from Mosiah are familiar to us:

"Behold, here are the waters of Mormon (for thus were they called) and now, as ye are desirous to come into the fold of God, and to be called his people, and are willing to bear one another's burdens, that they may be light; yea, and are willing to mourn with those that mourn; yea, and comfort those that stand in need of comfort, and to stand as witnesses of God at all times and in all things, and in all places that ye may be in, even until death, that ye may be redeemed of God, and be numbered with those of the first resurrection, that ye may have eternal life—now I say unto you, if this be the desire of your hearts, what have you against being baptized in the name of the Lord, as a witness before him that ye have entered into a covenant with him, that ye will serve him and keep his commandments, that he may pour out his Spirit more abundantly upon you? And now when the people had heard these words, they clapped their hands for joy, and exclaimed: This is the desire of our hearts" (Mosiah 18:8–11).

This is also the desire of *our* hearts, and I have noticed how frequently the service Latter-day Saints extend to those who mourn or stand in need of comfort takes tangible forms. I have been blessed to see kindnesses extended to people I love: homemade meals, thoughtful cards, shoveled walks, or flower arrangements that dispel a haze of loneliness and pain. These signs of kindness vanish, but they leave something vital in their place. Long after the casserole has been eaten, the driveway is snowed over again, and the flowers have wilted, the bonds of love between God's covenant children remain. There is nothing magic or transcendent about a meal, or a handwritten card, or a quilt— until it has been infused with the love of someone who extends, in faith, the kindness Christ would offer to the weary or the brokenhearted. Things are only things until they become tokens of covenant hearts. Then, when we offer them to others, things that don't keep can meet someone's immediate needs, and the light of faith and love those offerings generate can burn forever.

It is a remarkable feature of Christ's parable of the ten virgins that the wise virgins were those with *less* oil in their lamps than their foolish counterparts at the end of the story. Less oil, but more light. The parable, in Matthew, is as simple as it is profound:

"Then shall the kingdom of heaven be likened unto ten virgins, which took their lamps, and went forth to meet the bridegroom. And five of them were wise, and five were foolish. They that were foolish took their lamps, and took no oil with them: But the wise took oil in their vessels with their lamps. While the bridegroom tarried, they all slumbered and slept. And at midnight there was a cry made, Behold, the bridegroom cometh; go ye out to meet him. Then all those virgins arose, and trimmed their lamps. And the foolish said unto the wise, Give us of your oil; for our lamps are gone out. But the wise answered, saying, Not so; lest there be not enough for us and you: but go ye rather to them that sell, and buy for yourselves. And while they went to buy, the bridegroom came; and they that were ready went in with him to the marriage: and the door was shut. Afterward came also the other virgins, saying, Lord, Lord, open to us. But he answered and said, Verily I say unto you, I know you not. Watch therefore, for ye know neither the day nor the hour wherein the Son of man cometh" (Matthew 25:1–13).

The foolish virgins, unprepared for the sudden appearance of the Bridegroom, run to buy oil for their lamps—but too late. When they finally stand at the door with lamps full of newly-purchased oil, it turns out that a burning lamp, and not unused oil, qualifies one to join the Bridegroom. The oil of the wise virgins did not keep, but the light they created in *using* it illuminated their path to the Light that endures.

What does it mean, then, to be prepared to meet the Savior—to know Him when we see Him, and to feel He knows us? Christ, the master teacher, immediately follows this parable in Matthew with another that complements and further illuminates its message, placing greater emphasis on our charge to follow Him in blessing others. Taken together, these parables show the spiritual rewards that come from *combining* individual

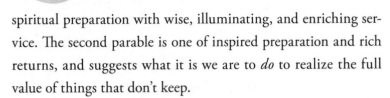

spiritual preparation with wise, illuminating, and enriching service. The second parable is one of inspired preparation and rich returns, and suggests what it is we are to *do* to realize the full value of things that don't keep.

Here is the story: Before leaving on a long journey, a man entrusts his servants with amounts of money consistent with their various abilities. The servant who receives the most money—five talents—invests the talents and earns five more. The servant who receives two talents also invests his, at an identical rate of return. But a third servant receives only one talent, which he promptly hides in the ground. Understandably, he acts out of fear. What would his master say if the talent were lost? But in trying to keep the coin, the servant has rendered it worthless. The real value is not in coin that is kept—but in talents that have been used, put to wise and fruitful purposes. When we use—rather than foolishly seek to save—the things of value in our lives, the Lord treats our offering as an investment, one which he matches and transforms into something of enduring worth (see Matthew 25:14–46).

A few weeks ago, I attended the funeral of my first visiting teaching companion. I knew her only in the last decade of her life. Her husband died a few years before I met her. For thirty-three years, she had suffered a painful and debilitating illness. Her health challenges notwithstanding, she was a legendary visiting teacher. She arranged all our appointments at the beginning of the month; all that was left to me was to pick her up and drive to the meetings. I saw the pain on her face as she struggled in and out of my car, but I saw, in her commitment to those visits and our care for those sisters, how much she valued her covenants to wear herself out in the Lord's service. One week she called me to let me know the date she'd arranged for the month's visit—a date that happened to be my birthday. I perceived this as a conflict; she suggested I perceive it as a gift. "It will be a happy birthday," she said. "Because you'll be serving someone." When I picked her up for our appointment, she was standing at the door with a homemade birthday cake perched on top of her walker. Her grandchildren who lived with her later told me they would often be awakened before six o'clock in the morning by a sound they called a "pan avalanche," as my companion tussled with the cookware she needed to do some good in the world. With a cake thus made on my birthday, she was prepared to transform our monthly visit into a party.

My companion's family knew that their untiring mother and grandmother would also want her funeral to be transformed into a meaningful service opportunity. And so, on tables outside the chapel doors, they arranged stacks of copies of the Book of Mormon inscribed with her testimony, intended as gifts for those who knew and loved her but were not members of the Church. The room was full of such people and others who had been blessed, lifted, and encouraged by a wise woman who bent every reserve of physical strength in her frail body to the task of bearing other people's burdens and comforting those who stood in need of comfort. Her grandchildren paid tribute to her life with the words of a song she loved: "I'm trying to love my neighbor; / I'm learning to serve my friends. / I watch for the day of gladness when Jesus will come again."[1] She dedicated herself wholly, even recklessly, to this work, often pushing the limits of her physical capacity. But on the tables outside the chapel, and in the faces of her children and grandchildren inside, I saw evidence of the light

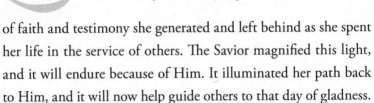

of faith and testimony she generated and left behind as she spent her life in the service of others. The Savior magnified this light, and it will endure because of Him. It illuminated her path back to Him, and it will now help guide others to that day of gladness.

In many ways, my dedicated visiting teaching companion reminds me of my own wise mother. Among the papers I found in her basement were notes to and from her children that chronicle how, in ways large and small, she illuminated our days and nights. She made sacrifices to keep this flame alive, but always with a winning combination of humor and faith. I remember one example: A note she left on the kitchen counter when she accompanied my father on a church assignment and left my teenaged older sister and me alone. She always faithfully accepted these Church assignments, but the absence from home they required tugged at a mother's heart. Nevertheless, she served with grace, wit, and warmth. The note she left on the counter has an arrow at the top, pointing left toward a pile of crumpled one-dollar bills and spare change, which she had obviously swept from her closet shelf. I could well believe that my mother, who rarely visited an ATM and almost never carried cash, spoke truthfully when she wrote below the arrow, "My entire life's savings I leave to my daughters Mary and Elizabeth," then on a new line, "But it will do them no good unless they take these," and a second arrow pointed right, to a bottle of vitamins. If we had some trouble procuring food with these meager funds, at least my sister and I had the vitamin pills to compensate and a mother's love to nourish us.

In fact, my mother left us a more enriching but less visible inheritance. If she required us to fend for ourselves occasionally, she spoiled us spiritually beyond my powers to appreciate. As a wise and vigilant mother, she had faith that the Lord would match her efforts. One of the papers I discovered in her basement records this expression of her testimony: "I am grateful that the Lord has answered our prayers in behalf of our children. I know that every blessing they receive comes from our Father in Heaven and His Son, Jesus Christ. Because I know that, it is easy for me to feel gratitude. I know that the blessings they receive come from God after I have done all that I can for them. It is easy to feel grateful when I realize that Heavenly Father and the Savior are the source of those blessings."

It is easy for me to feel grateful for a mother who did all a loving parent could possibly do for her children and then exercised faith that the Lord would reward her precious investment. In some sense, the boxes in her basement—full of testimonies likes these—contain receipts of the things she did not keep, the investments she made in faith and saw more than doubled by the Lord. My mother is a frugal woman in every sense except for the extravagance with which she invests in oil: continuously filling and burning a lamp of testimony. I see the Lord accept and magnify her offering, transforming what could have been a tiny light into a veritable pillar of fire with which she illuminates a path home to Him. In this extravagance, she is wise and generous.

She used to read me a familiar Christmas story about newlyweds who each sold their most treasured possession—he, a watch, and she, her long hair—to buy a gift for the other. Alas! He sold the watch to buy combs for the vanished hair, and she sold her hair to buy a chain for the pawned watch. How apparently foolish; how truly wise. The story ends this way: "The magi, as you know, were wise men—wonderfully wise men—who brought gifts to the

Babe in the manger. They invented the art of giving Christmas presents. Being wise, their gifts were no doubt wise ones, possibly bearing the privilege of exchange in case of duplication. And here I have lamely related to you the uneventful chronicle of two foolish children in a flat who most unwisely sacrificed for each other the greatest treasures of their house. But in a last word to the wise of these days let it be said that of all who give gifts these two were the wisest. Of all who give and receive gifts, such as they are wisest. Everywhere they are wisest. They are the magi."[2]

When my wise visiting teaching companion and my wise mother greet the Savior, they will be prepared to meet Him because they have become like Him. They have offered all they treasure out of love for Him. They have worn themselves out in His service. Matthew 25 begins with the parable of the ten virgins, and then relates Christ's parable of the talents, which I have shared. The chapter then closes with a glorious elucidation of what it means to be prepared, to be truly wise:

"When the Son of man shall come in his glory, and all the holy angels with him, then shall he sit upon the throne of his glory: and before him shall be gathered all nations: and he shall separate them one from another, as a shepherd divideth his sheep from the goats: and he shall set the sheep on his right hand, but the goats on the left. Then shall the King say unto them on his right hand, Come, ye blessed of my Father, inherit the kingdom prepared for you from the foundation of the world: for I was an hungred, and ye gave me meat: I was thirsty, and ye gave me drink: I was a stranger, and ye took me in: naked, and ye clothed me: I was sick, and ye visited me: I was in prison, and ye came unto me. Then shall the righteous answer him, saying, Lord, when saw we thee an hungred, and fed thee? or thirsty, and gave thee drink? when saw we thee a stranger, and took thee in? or naked, and clothed thee? or when saw we thee sick, or in prison, and came unto thee? And the King shall answer and say unto them, Verily I say unto you, Inasmuch as ye have done it unto one of the least of these my brethren, ye have done it unto me" (Matthew 25:31–40).

We spend our days toiling over a hundred things that don't keep—like meat, and drink, and clothing. But when we offer food, clothing, time, compassion, friendship, or love to God's children, the Lord magnifies our efforts and transforms the perishable into the eternal. A hundred small and fleeting kindnesses to others are eternally significant kindnesses to the Savior. Elder Jeffrey R. Holland spoke eloquently of the real and lasting power of such charity: "I am grateful for *all* the women of the Church who in my life have been as strong as Mount Sinai and as compassionate as the Mount of Beatitudes. We smile sometimes about our sisters' stories—you know, green Jell-O, quilts, and funeral potatoes. But my family has been the grateful recipient of each of those items at one time or another—and in one case, the quilt and the funeral potatoes on the same day. It was just a small quilt—tiny, really—to make my deceased baby brother's journey back to his heavenly home as warm and comfortable as our Relief Society sisters wanted him to be. The food provided for our family after the service, voluntarily given without a single word from us, was gratefully received. Smile, if you will, about our traditions, but somehow the too-often unheralded women in this church are *always* there when hands hang down and knees are feeble. They seem to grasp instinctively the divinity in

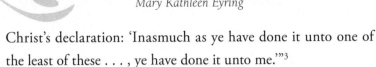

Christ's declaration: 'Inasmuch as ye have done it unto one of the least of these . . . , ye have done it unto me.'"[3]

I know the comfort and joy such service can bring to individuals and to families. In the boxes in the basement, I found mementos of a legacy of Christlike service handed down through generations of women in my family. My maternal grandmother's compassionate service to children in her community with particular challenges left a lasting impression on my mother, who often described this service to me. Some of my earliest memories are of performing musical numbers and visiting with residents in assisted-living centers. I had a sense even as a young child that these small and seemingly inconsequential activities were at the center of the life I wanted to live and the woman—like my mother and grandmother—I wanted to become. As they showed me the joy of service, these women taught me of the Savior.

On a scrap of paper which will not keep, my mother wrote this expression of faith which surely will endure. She delivered it at a conference several years ago: "Mary, our youngest daughter, is in California today. Her plan is to be with my mother in church in Menlo Park. My mother is ninety-five years old. She is in a wheelchair, but she is in Church every Sunday she can get there. My prayer is that she is there today with my daughter. My mother's example of faith blesses my life, is blessing my daughter's life, and will likely bless her posterity for generations to come. And the faith which takes her to meetings, even when it is so hard, fills her heart and mine with gratitude."

I come from a line of women who save tokens and receipts of things invested in the Lord's service, so it is not surprising that I do the same. Over ten years and throughout moves that have taken me to both American coasts and across the Atlantic, I have carried a note that says: "Mary, You light up my life. Love, Mom." It's almost miraculous that this slip of paper hasn't been lost in one of my many moves, and I certainly don't count on it surviving many more. But I will cherish its sentiment forever. If I am or have been a light in anyone's life, it is because my mother led me toward the source of all light. I will be eternally grateful that she taught me through example that nothing has real or lasting value in this life except for the things we offer to the Savior in His service—and which he magnifies and transforms into things that endure. I hope, like the wise virgins of the parable, that I will be prepared to meet the Bridegroom with a diminished oil reserve wisely invested over a lifetime of illuminated discipleship.

I am grateful for the things in life we do not keep, but use and burn and invest in service to God's children—and thus in service to the Savior Himself. I have a testimony of the gospel of Jesus Christ. He is the Light of the world. And I have a testimony that when we use all that we have and all that we cherish to fulfill the covenants we make at baptism, we prepare ourselves for a day of gladness, when we will meet the Savior, and He will say: "Well done, thou good and faithful servant: thou hast been faithful over a few things, I will make thee ruler over many things: enter thou into the joy of thy lord" (Matthew 25:21, 23).

The Safety, Comfort, and Peace of Jesus

Laurel Christensen Day

In the spring of 2014, I found myself in London with my husband and eighteen-year-old stepson. And while the trip was magical in so many ways, it was actually the time we spent at Westminster Abbey that proved to be the experience that will linger with me for a very long time.

Prior to the trip, my friend Fiona Givens had told me that not only did we need to allow plenty of time for the visit to Westminster, she also strongly encouraged us to attend the evening choir performance, or "evensong," which is part of their daily worship service. I have attended worship services of many faiths throughout my life. You might say it's a bit of an odd hobby for me. I have often felt the Spirit while worshipping alongside my friends of other faiths. And this service was no different. It was Easter week, and amidst the recitation and the singing and the kneeling and the standing, I felt a deep love for my Savior within that historic building. And as the service concluded, I found myself listening intently to every word of the benediction.

After the "amen," I couldn't get a pen out fast enough to

write down these words from the priest's prayer: "In His wounds may we find safety. In His scars may we find comfort. In His pain may we find peace."

Those inviting words stayed with me the next few days of our trip and proved to be the catalyst to an expansion of my understanding of the Atonement of Jesus Christ.

Elder Jeffrey R. Holland taught, "The Atonement of the Only Begotten Son of God in the flesh is the crucial foundation upon which all Christian doctrine rests and the greatest expression of divine love the world has ever been given." And then he added, "Every other principle, commandment, and virtue of the restored gospel draws its significance from this pivotal event."[1]

Drawing upon the beautiful words of that prayer at Westminster Abbey, let's explore three ways I believe we can experience the greatest expression of divine love that is the Atonement of Jesus Christ.

FIRST: FIND SAFETY IN HIS WOUNDS

Jude, in his one short epistle in the New Testament, refers to the Savior as "him that is able to keep you from falling" (Jude 1:24). Can you feel the truth of that statement? Can you recall a time when He has kept you from falling? Do you see that He does so, even today in this very hour?

Elder Holland taught this truth perhaps more beautifully than I have ever heard it expressed in the April 2015 general conference. He told the story of two brothers, Jimmy and John, who attempted to scale a sheer canyon wall in Snow Canyon. They found themselves stranded on a ledge. After the older brother, John, boosted his younger brother Jimmy to safety, John found himself in a life-threatening situation without anything to hold onto. Just as he jumped up to take hold of anything that might allow him to save himself, his younger brother was there to grab his arms and hold onto his brother. He refused to let him fall and Jimmy lifted his brother John to safety.

Elder Holland then expressed deep appreciation for the Savior, Jesus Christ, whose "brotherly hands and determined arms . . . reached into the abyss of death to save us from our fallings and our failings, from our sorrows and our sins."[2]

In Isaiah 53:5 we read, "But he was wounded for our transgressions, he was bruised for our iniquities" (see also Mosiah 14:5). The Savior's wounds are evidence of his suffering. That suffering occurred to provide what I see as a safety net for our lives. Because of Christ's atoning sacrifice, we will not be lost. There is nothing we can do—save the unpardonable sin—that will separate us from the safety that His mercy provides. Because of Him, we will not fall. We have a protection as we "learn from our own experience" in this mortal journey.

I think we forget that. I think we forget that our Father's plan provides for our safety—and that safety comes through the Atonement that is there to "save us from our fallings and our failings, from our sorrows *and* our sins," just as Elder Holland taught. Our Father wants us back. *He wants us back!* And the Atonement of Jesus Christ actually makes that possible. Yes, we have covenants to make and keep. Jacob teaches us in 2 Nephi 9 that Christ can then deliver us from "that awful monster the devil, and death, and hell, and that lake of fire and brimstone"

(v. 19) so we can be "restored to that God who gave [us] breath, which is the Holy One of Israel" (v.26). What a promise!

Truly in His wounds we can find safety.

SECOND: FIND COMFORT IN HIS SCARS

A scar is defined as "the lasting aftereffect of trouble." A scar could also be said to be something that cannot be changed (or will not be changed) in this life. With that definition as a background, I would invite you to think about the scars you might have or the aftereffects of mortality you might be dealing with.

The prints of the nails in His hands and in His feet are the Savior's scars—left as a reminder of the cross and as evidence of what He did for all of God's children. That suffering and taking upon himself our sins and our pains gives Him the ability to comfort us. The priest offering the beautiful prayer at Westminster said, "In His scars may we find comfort"—and what my spirit heard was, "And in *your* scars, Laurel, may you find comfort." Or in other words, "In the things in your life that cannot be changed, may you find comfort."

The prophet Isaiah taught, "For the Lord shall comfort Zion: he will comfort all her waste places; and he will make her wilderness like Eden, and her desert like the garden of the Lord; joy and gladness shall be found therein, thanksgiving, and the voice of melody" (Isaiah 51:3). He will comfort us. He will make our wilderness like Eden. He will make our desert places like a garden. He will make our scars, those things that will not be changed in this life, beautiful.

I grew up, like most girls, with plans and dreams for one thing: being a mom to children of my own. And I was going to have a houseful. So there was perhaps nothing more painful in my late thirties (not even my single status at the time) than watching that dream go unrealized. This situation caused me to spend a lot of time in prayer. One prayer experience led me to learn a powerful principle. I call it the "principle of enough."

I was getting ready to petition the Lord once again for the desires of my heart but for some reason I felt that the things I was getting ready to pray for weren't right. It's not that they weren't righteous or worthy—they just weren't right. And instead I sensed I needed to pray for something else.

"Make it enough." I heard myself say and I must have said it three or four times. And then, while still in prayer, I thought of the miracle of the loaves and the fishes.

"Make it enough," my spirit said. "Please make what you have for me enough right now."

While still kneeling, I grabbed my scriptures and found myself in Matthew 14. And then the accounts of the same event recorded by Mark . . . and Luke . . . and John. I discovered something that had a powerful effect on me. I think I always thought the five loaves and the two small fishes were multiplied in order to make them enough. But it doesn't actually say that.

- Matthew 14:20—"And they did all eat, and were filled."
- Mark 6:41—"And the two fishes divided he among them all."
- Luke 9:16—"He took the five loaves and the two fishes, and looking up to heaven, he blessed them."
- John 6:14—They saw "the miracle that Jesus did."

I noticed something in that story I had never seen before: What if it wasn't about the Lord giving them more? Maybe He did. Maybe He did actually give them more. But that's not what I read in those scriptures. Instead, what I read and felt was that He took what they had, He took what was there, and just made it *enough*—enough to satisfy their need.

It was such a profound truth and it changed the way I prayed during those trying times. I still petitioned the Lord for my righteous desires but I also often found myself asking the Lord to make what He had for me enough.

And He did. And He has.

You see, I did not marry until 2013 at the age of forty-one, and one of the ironies of my life is that I was given one deeply desired hope of my heart a little too late to have the blessing of another: children of my own, a posterity. It is not in the cards for me and I think a part of me always knew that it wasn't. It has been the source of more hurt in this life than I can adequately express. You might say it is one of my scars.

However, with this marriage came four stepsons. I love these men. And they have been gracious to me. But it was the youngest (the eighteen-year-old who was with us at Westminster Abbey) whom the Lord used to solidify this "principle of enough" for me.

I would have never imagined that this boy, who has only been in my life for a few years, who doesn't need a mother because he has a great one, who in many ways had little use for me but chose to let me into his life—I could have never imagined that being his stepmom would feel like enough. But in so many ways, it has. And only God (and now perhaps my husband) knows what a miracle that is—how a couple of years has satisfied a lifetime of wanting. That is a miracle!

Now, this is not to say that there are not moments that the reality of this particular scar still overcomes my little heart with sadness. But I have found great comfort in a situation that should not have been enough to comfort me. And this is truly one of the mercies of the Atonement: He is able to take five fishes and two loaves of bread (or one stepson) and make them enough. He takes those things that cannot be changed for us in this life—our scars, our wildernesses, our deserts—and makes them our Eden, our garden, our enough.

In our scars, we find His comfort.

Third: Find Peace in His Pain

In the Book of Mormon, Jacob taught us that the Savior "suffereth the pains of all men, yea, the pains of every living creature, both men, women, and children, who belong to the family of Adam" (2 Nephi 9:21).

He felt our pains—not just from our sin, but the pain that is a result of life's disappointments and heartaches. The pain we feel as mothers of rebellious children; the pain we feel as women who wish we had children to be rebellious. The pain of being single; the pain of women in troubled marriages who sometimes wish they were. The pain of betrayal. The pain of loss. He experienced all of that pain.

And in a way I had not thought about prior to that prayer at Westminster Abbey and that I do not understand, His pain allows for Him to provide peace to the world. The scriptures teach us that "the chastisement of our peace was upon him; and with his stripes we are healed" (Isaiah 53:5; see also Mosiah 14:5).

I am a witness of the reality that the Atonement provides peace amidst pain.

About fifteen years ago, when my sister and her husband had two young children, an opportunity arose to foster twin newborns and they took it. It was the intention and their understanding that the foster care was the means to adopt them (which would likely happen after a year). My sister's first two children were the products of adoption, so she and her husband were fairly comfortable with the process.

I was able to spend some time in their home just weeks after the twins arrived. I remember staying up late with one twin so my sister could try and get some sleep before the other awoke. It was an exhausting and amazing week. I was immediately in love with these sweet little boys.

That first year, we loved these babies. We had vacation time with them. We took family pictures with them. They were as much a part of our family as any children could be. And we were excited as the year mark approached.

Then the news came that the boys might be reunited with their birth family. That should be happy news, I suppose; children should get to be with their birth family whenever possible. The problem was that the situation they were being returned to was not a good one. And the boys *were* with their family—they were with us.

We all talked about fasting and praying and petitioning the Lord for a miracle. I remember telling my family that I couldn't recall a single time we had ever asked for a miracle; surely the

Lord would grant a request like this. Staying in our family meant these boys would have the gospel of Jesus Christ. Staying in our family meant the hope of a life filled with Primary and youth conference and missions and the temple.

So we fasted and prayed. And I remember one night sincerely telling the Lord that if my sister could have these boys, I would even forego the blessing of the children He might have in store for me. Those words actually came out of my mouth. And I meant every word. This miracle was that important.

And then, right around the time of their first birthday, my sister and her husband were told to return those boys to the care of the state. The boys were gone. And I. Was. Devastated.

God had not granted our request. He had not listened to my plea. He had not intervened.

I spent the next year or so feeling very distanced from Deity. I was very guarded in my prayers. I had decided I didn't want to set myself up for that kind of heartbreak again.

About a year after we lost the twins, I found myself sitting in a church meeting. The speaker shared her own story of little baby twins dealing with health issues and said that the prospects for survival did not look good. So the family fasted and prayed for a miracle. My heart started to sink. I'm embarrassed to admit what I sat there and silently thought: "Please have the story end with the loss of the twins. Please don't let them live."

I so desperately needed a message of "sometimes it doesn't work—sometimes God does not grant the miracle."

But the story ended. And the family got their miracle. And although the speaker then referred to times when things don't work out like they did for them, I heard nothing but "God grants needed miracles. He just doesn't grant yours."

There, in an instant, in a gathering of thousands, I was entirely alone. The downward spiral that had begun a year prior was now in freefall. I was numb. I felt completely empty.

It was a few weeks later that I found myself teaching the children in Primary. We were discussing the gospel principle of fasting and prayer. It was sharing time for the seven- to eleven-year-olds. I was in the midst of a major faith crisis and had no business teaching that Sunday.

I wasn't prepared for the question from one young boy. His older brother was home from his mission on medical leave and he asked, "Sister Christensen, how come when we fasted and prayed for my brother Sam, he didn't get better?"

I couldn't answer Gavin's question. I knew all the *right* answers. But I didn't have the *real* one.

"Well, Gavin, what do you think?"

"I don't know."

"Maybe you didn't fast long enough?" I heard myself say.

"No, we fasted for a long time."

"Hmmm . . . maybe you didn't pray hard enough?" I responded.

"No, we prayed hard a lot."

"Maybe you don't really want it?" I questioned.

"No, we do. We want him to get better."

"Well, maybe God isn't listening." I'm sure the other adults in the room were wondering where I was headed with that risky statement. Frankly, I was wondering too.

"No, He is listening. He's always listening," Gavin replied

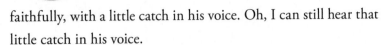

faithfully, with a little catch in his voice. Oh, I can still hear that little catch in his voice.

"Well, Gavin, if you fasted long enough and prayed hard enough and you really want it and God is listening, maybe God just doesn't want Sam to get better."

"No, he has to want Sam to get better. He has to."

It was as if time stood still as I heard Gavin say those words. I felt in my heart my Father had heard my prayer too and wanted me to "get better." He wanted to heal the pain in my heart. But I was at a loss. I stood there paralyzed, not sure where this discussion was going or what I should say next.

"Please, Father. Please," I silently cried out from somewhere deep in my heart. "Please help Gavin . . . please help me."

And then I asked what proved to be the all-important question: "Can anyone tell us why Sam isn't getting better even though Gavin and his family are fasting and praying?"

Well, that's what came out of my mouth, but my real question was: "Can someone please tell me why the Lord hasn't responded to my pleas? My heart is breaking. I feel alone. I'm at the edge of my faith. Please help me."

And, for as long as I live, I will remember little eight-year-old Jonathan. "Sister Christensen?" Jonathan said while raising his hand. I looked at him and it seemed Jonathan, as if speaking for the Lord Himself, spoke right to my heart: "Maybe because sometimes the answer is no."

And in that moment, time *did* stand still. I know it did. The room froze. And the Spirit infused in my heart a profound truth about my life and God's dealings with me and His love for me. And I understood something new about the healing power of the

Atonement because I felt it immediately. After a year of pain and struggle, I experienced an instant healing. I was at peace.

In His final days of his life, Jesus said: "Peace I leave with you, my peace I give unto you: not as the world giveth, give I unto you. Let not your heart be troubled" (John 14:27). Because of His pain and in the midst of ours, we can find peace.

While touring the halls of Westminster Abbey, I was in awe at the memorials and burial epitaphs: Mary, Queen of Scots; Sir Isaac Newton; Alfred, Lord Tennyson; Charles Darwin. We were surrounded by the remains of so many people who have made an impact on the history of the world.

And then I saw a little stone with these words inscribed: "Here lies the body of Philip Clark, 'Plumber' to this Collegiate Church. . . . He departed this life 21st of September 1707, in the 43rd year of his age." I loved that I was in a place that seemed like God might actually be a respecter of persons until I saw this reminder that even when man is, He is not.

And the atoning sacrifice of the Savior Jesus Christ is not a respecter of persons either.

While I do not understand the laws that allow the Atonement to be the means of safety and comfort and peace in our lives, I know with all my heart that it is. And that truth helps me understand more deeply how the Atonement truly is "the greatest expression of divine love the world has ever been given." May you feel of that divine love as you find safety in His wounds, comfort through His scars, and peace amidst your pain.

"Help Thou Mine Unbelief"

Fiona Givens

I am a non-linear thinker, which means that while we shall, as it were, all go on a walk into the wood, we may or may not come out. We may take a variety of paths, some of which may lead nowhere. There are advantages, however, to non-linear thinking: My deficiencies relieve you of any obligation to take notes.

I would like to start in D&C 46. In it we find a wonderful reminder of gifts. We'll start in verse 11: "For all have not every gift given unto them; for there are many gifts, and to every man [and every woman] is given a gift by the Spirit of God. To some is given one, and to some is given another, that all may be profited thereby. To some it is given by the Holy Ghost to *know* that Jesus Christ is the Son of God, and that he was crucified for the sins of the world. To others it is given to *believe* on their words, that they also might have eternal life if they continue faithful" (D&C 46:11–14).

Particularly interesting is that God does not distinguish between the two gifts *knowledge* and *belief*. It appears that knowledge and belief are gifts of equal value. And in fact, belief might be more helpful than knowledge on our faith journey because it allows room for doubt and, therefore, choice. President Hugh B. Brown (quoting Will Durant) said, "No one deserves to believe unless [he or she] has served an apprenticeship in doubt."[1] Doubt can be a crucial time for realignment in our lives—a period of necessary education, a clarion call to rouse our spirits and push against the walls that threaten to engulf us.

The focus in this beautiful scripture we have been given to discuss (Mark 9:24) is on a distraught father—I'd like to spend a little time with him. One has the feeling that this father, who has spent years and years seeking a cure for his son, has exhausted every single possible recourse. He's gone to every healer, to every person he can possibly imagine—including Christ's disciples—and very possibly expended a great deal of money in search of a remedy for the dreadful malady that has, for years, tortured his son. I also have the feeling that his coming to Christ was the last resort. He had nowhere else to go. He entreats the Savior, "Have compassion on us, and help us" (Mark 9:22). The words are an entreaty from a parent in agony. Every time his son is attacked, his father suffers the brunt of the assault, incapable as he is of protecting his child. Perhaps the question Christ then asks is not so much directed to the child's father as it is to His apostles, whom He has just reproved for their inability to cast out the malignant spirit—the lack of faith of those who, unlike the father, have witnessed Christ's power to heal for so long. He turns to the father, looking deeply into his eyes, touching him no doubt, as was his wont, and suggests, "If thou canst believe, all things are possible" (Mark 9:23). The father wants desperately to believe. Perhaps because, in spite of the pain, he senses in Christ the power to heal that he cries out the words given him by the Savior: "Lord, I believe." But the lifelong battle with fear, rejection, and disappointment are much more powerful than this fragile, nascent stirring in his heart and mind. Sensing his longing to believe being swamped by the omnipresent terror, he entreats the Lord for aid: "Help thou mine unbelief" (Mark 9:24). He looks back into Christ's eyes and he knows that Christ has seen that he cannot believe. Belief is beyond his power.

The father neither knows nor is capable of believing that the Man standing before him is the promised Messiah. And what is Christ's response to the desperate plea of the man who lacks both knowledge and belief? He heals his son. He heals his son. And in so doing, the Savior of the World answers the father's desperate prayer, "Help thou mine unbelief." Why? We have already ascertained that the father is not able to believe. Could it be that the Savior heals simply out of compassion for the father and the son? *Compassion* is from the Latin: *com* (with) and *passion* (suffer). Looking into the desperate eyes of this father, did not the Lord also feel the desperation that he felt? Was He not moved by love for this man and his anguish? And Jesus, after casting out the malevolent spirit, took the child "by the hand, and lifted him up; and he arose" (Mark 9:27).

The *Lectures on Faith* state that "in order that any rational and intelligent being may exercise faith in God unto life and salvation [we need to know not only] that He exists [but also to have] a *correct* idea of his character, perfections, and attributes."[2] Such an interesting idea. Joseph doesn't simply say that we need to *know* God's character. He inserts the word *correct*, which, of course, implies that there are *incorrect* characteristics attributed to God in the canon. If people wish to learn about the God of Christianity, it is more than likely that they will be directed to the Bible. However, the Book of Mormon states that during the process of Biblical redaction "*many* parts which are plain and precious" have been removed (1 Nephi 13:26; emphasis added).

To my mind the most plain and precious thing that has been removed from the biblical text is the compassionate God whom Christ emulates in this story. True, the God of compassion is to be seen in the Old Testament—but you have to search for Him. The God of wrath, vengeance, and destruction dominates the Biblical narrative. Have you seen the film of the musical *Les Misérables*?[3] Do you remember that very unsettling scene at the beginning of the film where the director has Javert walking so close to the edge that you're wondering if the director has actually read the book and if he knows that Javert isn't supposed to die at the beginning of the film? And then we get to the crucial scene of the film— Javert's suicide, which I think the director, Tom Hooper, managed brilliantly. Again Inspector Javert is walking along another precarious ledge as he had done in the opening scene.

His whole world has just been upended because Jean Valjean has saved his life. This is not possible in his paradigm. In Javert's world, God is incapable of aiding people to transition from bad to good, from unbelief to belief. For Javert worships a wrathful, vengeful god, a god who demands sacrifice and pain and suffering for every single sin. Every centime you have lost or stolen must be repaid fourfold. And as he is walking that precipice, we recognize that what we are witnessing is a contestation between the two gods—the angry, vengeful god of Javert and the merciful, benevolent, longsuffering, infinitely patient, compassionate God of Jean Valjean. And in taking his own life, Javert symbolically takes the life of the wrathful, vengeful god. For, as Julian of Norwich wrote, "It is the most unpossible that may be that God shulde be wrath. For wrath and frenschyppe [friendship] be two contrarioese [contraries]."[4] It is the Prophet Joseph who reclaimed the God of friendship and compassionate love.

In the nineteenth century, the god of Jonathan Edwards ruled supreme in this country and that same god ruled pretty much over most of Christianity and beyond. When God first appears to Joseph in the Sacred Grove, the Lord says, "their creeds are an abomination before me" (Joseph Smith–History 1:19)—to which creeds is God referring? Due to the prevalent anti-Catholic sentiment of much of our Mormon past, we have long assumed that the Catholic creeds were the "abomination" to which the Lord is referring. However, upon closer examination, it is more likely to be the Westminster Confessions and the Thirty-Nine Articles of the Church of England—the Protestant creeds—for it is they that declare that God is a God without body, without parts and, most importantly, without passions. (It was to those creeds that Joseph afterwards frequently referred; it is unlikely he would even have known the Catholic creeds.) In other words, God could not be moved by human suffering. He lacked compassion.[5] As the Protestant creeds are based on an understanding of God's character and attributes found in the Bible, it is to the Restoration texts we must look for scriptures that restore the "plain and precious thing"—God's compassion.

Jacob 5, for example, is one of the longest chapters in the Book of Mormon. It comprises seventy-seven verses—all of which could be summarized in three. What is repeated again and again is the length to which God is willing to go to save each of his olive trees. The leitmotif that flows throughout is "it grieveth me." "It grieveth me that I should lose [*this tree*]" (see vv. 7, 11, 13, 32, 46, 47, 51, and 66). So concerned is he for every single one of the trees in the olive grove that he goes to the nethermost parts of the grove, to the hopeless, the helpless, the corrupted and the lonely, the despairing, the marginalized, those who have lost loved ones, their belief, the ability to hang on in the face of so much darkness. The lesson of Jacob 5 is this: In choosing to set His heart upon us—to love us—God deliberately makes Himself vulnerable to our pain. How many of us in this room have loved? And how many of us have lost? Sigmund Freud correctly stated: "We are never so defenseless against suffering as when we love."[6]

Perhaps the most dramatic rendition of the cost of Heavenly love is to be found in Moses 7. After ascending to Heaven with his city, Zion, the prophet Enoch is more than a little discomfited. Instead of the joyful reception he had, no doubt, anticipated, Enoch notices, perhaps with some chagrin, that God's emotional energy and focus remain earthbound. Man of Holiness—God the Father—is weeping tears of grief. So unanticipated is this display of suffering that Enoch asks God, not once but three times: "How is it that thou canst weep, seeing thou art holy, and from all eternity to all eternity?" (Moses 7:28, 29, 31). And God answers, "Wherefore should not the heavens weep, seeing these [my other children] shall [continue to] suffer?" (Moses 7:37).

Beloved sisters, we worship a God who chose to set his

heart upon us. And in so doing, became vulnerable to our suffering. And herein lies his power to draw us all, His suffering children, home to the eternal embrace of our Heavenly Parents. As the brilliant and courageous theologian Dietrich Bonhoeffer stated, "Only the suffering God. . . . wins power and space in the world."[7] This is the "plain and precious thing" that was lost. This is the God whom Christ was emulating in his encounter with the desperate, suffering father and his malady-ridden child.

I am sure many, if not all of us, have loved ones who are suffering from a variety of causes. We may be attempting to carry their burdens as well as our own. Some of our children have drifted away from the Church disenchanted by the discovery of an unfamiliar history or theology. Some struggle with depression or any number of ailments, as did one of my sons. For a variety of reasons, he slipped onto a path injurious to himself and to his family. And yet, and yet . . . God was aware of my son and was working with him all the while. I was only aware of my failings as a mother, recalling, ad nauseam, the family home evenings that were missed or the family scripture study skipped, heaping recrimination upon my own head until, exhausted, I found myself on the road to the temple. On my return home, I felt that I was asked a number of questions, the last of which was, "Have you loved the children I sent you with all your heart?" Without the slightest hesitation, I could answer the question in a resounding affirmative—my failures notwithstanding. I have loved my children with all my heart. I was then reminded that this was all I that was required to do, and that the Lord would continue the journey with my son, who is also His son. But I was given some homework to do. I was asked to visit the temple more frequently and to fast often on behalf of my child. And the months passed—many of them.

Until one evening when the house was still and quiet and devoid of all its regular inhabitants and visitors—I was prompted to call my son. When he picked up, I immediately heard the catch in his voice, signaling that something was seriously amiss. Among other things, he told me that he saw nothing beautiful anymore, either in the world or in himself. Alarmed, I opened my mouth and spoke. And spoke, and spoke, and spoke; I have no idea what I spoke. Words just poured out. It was months later that my child returned home. Weeks passed, and one evening, as we were sitting on the veranda chatting, he asked, "Do you remember the night you called me?" I remembered it very clearly. He continued, "I don't remember what you said, but you spoke beautiful things to me." In time—in time the Lord leads each of His children home. Our scriptures attest that not only does Our Father expend considerable effort to ensure that we can return Home, but that He will never give up until we are all, once again, Home.

This is the glorious plan of the gospel of Jesus Christ. The Good News is that our Heavenly Parents have created a plan of happiness and salvation, whereby the entire human family can return home to Them. Doctrine and Covenants 121 expands our understanding of God's divine attributes and character: God is gentle, kind, longsuffering, infinitely patient, filled with love unfeigned—love unconditional—love without end (see D&C 121:41–42). Time is no barrier to our God; time is no barrier.

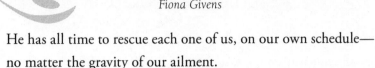

He has all time to rescue each one of us, on our own schedule—no matter the gravity of our ailment.

I do believe the Lord enlists each of us to help each other on our journeys. We are the benefactors of a beautiful baptismal covenant, delineated in Mosiah 18, which I would like to explore with you (see Mosiah 18:8–10).

At our baptism we make three covenants. The first covenant we make is to carry each other's burdens. I'm a very visual person, so when I hear the scripture, "Take up [your] cross, and follow me" (Mark 8:34), I picture us all carrying our cross and following Christ, who carries His cross. Every single one of us is carrying a cross—without exception. There is pain, loss, grief, psychological and physical impairment with which we are struggling. Visualize this with me. We're all spread out following the Savior with His cross, trudging behind Him, and one of us stumbles and falls under the weight of her cross. The person closest turns to help her lift her burden. But in order to lift her burden, the woman has to reach down and touch the cross her sister is carrying. It is only then that the full weight of the burden under which the sister is struggling is understood. Only in helping to lift her cross do we feel its weight.

The proffering of platitudes does not work—at all. When our pain is real and deep, when we have stumbled and are sitting in the road with our cross, it does not help to be told by those still trudging along to read the scriptures more often, to pray more often, to go to the temple more often. Grief that deep requires deep compassion, which is the second covenant we make: to mourn with her. It is only when we have felt and understood grief ourselves that we are capable of mourning. And mourning is grieving. And in grieving with our sister we are engaged in *compassion*. We "suffer with" her. It is then that we are able to take upon ourselves the third covenant. Because we now understand the nature of our sister's suffering, we are in a position—as Christ was with the desperate father—to offer comfort that is real, deep, and palpable.

The Savior comforted the father by healing his son. We comfort each other in so many ways as we open our hearts to the gentle instructions of the Holy Spirit. It is only then, really, that we "stand as witnesses of God," and bear testimony of Him who shall come to "dry up all tears" (Revelation 7:17; 21:4).

In all of our pain and suffering, it is helpful to recognize that we are not alone and that there are those around us who need us, that the person sitting next to you is suffering, and if we are able to develop that compassion, we become participators with Christ in the great healing process of mankind. We become co-participants with Christ, "Saviors on Mount Zion."

We are so fortunate to be members of this church, to be participants in the gospel of Jesus Christ. May I leave you with my favorite quote from the book of Romans: "For I am persuaded, that neither death, nor life, nor angels, nor principalities, nor powers, nor things present, nor things to come, nor height, nor depth, nor any other creature, shall be able to separate us from the love of God, which is in Christ Jesus our Lord" (Romans 8:39).

Repentance: A Fresh View
Kathryn Louise Callister

When my husband and I were assigned to work in the Pacific Area of the Church, we visited a sliver of an island by the name of Tarawa, part of the island nation of Kiribati. Most of the residents of that remote atoll rely on the sea for their sustenance. While there we visited a less-active family consisting of a returned-missionary father, a mother, and four sweet children. Their simple home was located right on the ocean. As my husband visited with this dear family, the Spirit filled the room, and the father, obviously touched, said, "My boat has been headed in the wrong direction. Today I will change the direction of my sails." The next day we were thrilled to see the entire family, with big smiles on their faces, at the stake conference.

Sisters, that is what repentance is all about: changing the "direction of our sails" or, in other words, the direction of our lives toward God. In Ezekiel we read, "Repent, and turn yourselves from all your transgressions; . . . and make you a new heart and a new spirit" (Ezekiel 18:30–31). Alma calls it "a mighty change [of] heart" (Alma 5:12), and the Bible Dictionary "a fresh view about God, about oneself, and about the world."[1]

Often we think of repentance in negative terms, but that is incorrect. It is a beautiful doctrine that is intertwined with the Atonement of our Savior. President Joseph Fielding Smith stated, "Repentance is one of the most comforting and glorious principles taught in the gospel."[2]

When we served our mission in Toronto, Canada, I sometimes worried about how our investigators would react to being taught that they needed to repent. I felt it sounded harsh to tell a wonderful investigator, who was basically a very good person, to repent. After all, I reasoned, such an investigator had not previously had the light of the gospel.

I thought of my dear father who was a convert to the Church at the age of thirty-three. I admired and loved him dearly and could not imagine missionaries asking my father, who was perfect in my eyes, to repent. He was so good, so kind, and so gentle I could not think of him ever having done anything of which to repent. Obviously, I did not understand the true nature of repentance—it is not just to correct us, but also to perfect us. President Gordon B. Hinckley said the gospel "is designed to . . . make good men better."[3]

How grateful I am that, years ago during World War II, my father took the missionary lessons, accepted the gospel, including the doctrine of repentance, and was baptized at Temple Beach near the Laie Hawaii Temple. He began leading an even more Christlike life of discipleship and service, became a valiant priesthood holder, took us to the temple, and became the father of an eternal family.

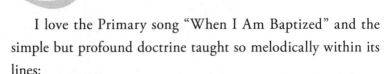

I love the Primary song "When I Am Baptized" and the simple but profound doctrine taught so melodically within its lines:

> I like to look for rainbows whenever there is rain
> And ponder on the beauty of an earth made clean again.
> I want my life to be as clean as earth right after rain.
> I want to be the best I can and live with God again.
> I know when I am baptized my wrongs are washed away,
> And I can be forgiven and improve myself each day.[4]

Can't you visualize rainbows, a clean earth, and the joy of our lives being made clean again through repentance? Because of the Atonement, we *can* feel as clean as "earth right after rain." Elder Richard G. Scott has said, "Which of us is not in need of the miracle of repentance?"[5] and, "Don't live your life in despair, feeling sorry for yourself because of the mistakes you have made. Let the sunshine in by doing the right things—now."[6]

Repentance is a change of heart and mind evidenced by recognition, Godly sorrow, forsaking sin, restitution, and confession. Sometimes the question is asked, "When is it necessary to confess to an appropriate priesthood leader?" Priesthood leaders have suggested, "When the sin is of such serious magnitude that it may trigger a disciplinary proceeding or continues to linger in our mind so that we cannot have peace."[7]

Elder Vaughn J. Featherstone told the story of a couple who finally decided to let that "sunshine in" by confessing a sin they had committed many years earlier. He relates, "A man knocked on my office door late at night and said, 'President, may I speak with you? Are we all alone?' I assured him no one else was in the office. We sat, . . . and he said, 'Four times I have driven over to the stake office and have seen your light on, and four times I have driven back home. . . . But, . . . last night I was reading in *The Miracle of Forgiveness* again, and I realized that every major transgression must be confessed. I have come to confess. . . . I have been on two high councils and have served as a bishop twice, and I believe the Lord called me.'

"I agreed, 'I'm sure he called you.'

"He said, 'Forty-two years ago, before my wife and I were married, we [engaged in serious immorality] once, the week prior to our going to the temple. We did not lie to the bishop, who was my wife's father; he simply talked with us and signed our recommends. We then went to the stake president, and he did not interview us. He signed our recommends, and we went to the temple unworthily. . . . We decided to make it up to the Lord. . . . We would pay more than our share of tithing and more than our share of building fund; we would accept every assignment to the welfare farm and do all else we were asked to do. We decided we were not worthy to go to the temple, and we did not go for a year. It has been forty-two years since the transgression, and we have lived as near Christlike lives as we know how. I believe we have been forgiven, but I know that confession is necessary.'

". . . Then he said, 'I would rather confess to you now. I am not a young man, and I do not have a lot of years left. I want to be able to meet my Savior with nothing left undone.'

"I listened to his confession. I wept with him, and when he finished . . . , I told him on behalf of the Church that he was

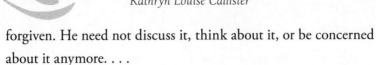

forgiven. He need not discuss it, think about it, or be concerned about it anymore. . . .

"We got up and walked to the door together. I said, 'Where is your wife?'

"He said, 'She is in the car.'

"I asked, 'Is she coming in?'

"He replied, 'No, she can't even think about it except it almost destroys her.'

"I said, 'You tell your wife that I would like to visit with her now. Tell her I want to take this off her heart and close it. . . .'

"He said, 'I'll tell her, but I don't think she will come in.'

"I answered, 'You tell her that if I have to sit here all night, I will not go home until she comes in. I can't bear the thought of her carrying this on her heart one more day in this life; forty-two years is long enough.'

"He said, 'Well, I'll tell her, but I don't think she'll come in.'

"He left and was gone fifteen minutes, thirty minutes, and forty-five minutes. . . . Then I heard a timid knock. . . . I went to the door, and there was this sweet woman standing there. Her eyes were wet from crying. . . . I took her by both hands and led her across the room. [We] sat . . . then I said, 'Your husband confessed to a transgression that happened over forty-two years ago of which you were a part. . . . You tell me, and I will take it off your heart.'

". . . Finally, about fifteen minutes later, she confessed. I wept; she wept. . . . Then I stood up . . . and we walked down the long hallway to the parking lot. . . . I said, 'How do you feel?'

"She stopped, looked up at me and, with tears in her eyes, said, *'President, I feel clean for the first time in forty-two years.'"*[8]

President Henry B. Eyring related a similar experience. He said, "I recall being in the temple with a couple [to] whom I had given recommends. Just as the ceremony was being performed, I had a pang of doubt. How could anyone who had done what one of them had be there? How could it be fair to the other?" And then he said, "I felt absolute assurance that the couple were as pure and clean as little children."[9]

Because of the Atonement, and through repentance, we *can* be clean again.

Though it is difficult, we have received beautiful and profound promises that we *can* change and be forgiven. President Boyd K. Packer has explained, "There is no habit, no addiction, no rebellion, no transgression, no offense exempted from the promise of complete forgiveness."[10]

Truman Madsen, a religious scholar at Brigham Young University, spoke similarly: "If there are some of you who have been tricked into the conviction that you have gone too far, that you have been weighed down with doubts on which you alone have a monopoly, that you have had the poison of sin that makes it impossible ever again to be what you could have been—then hear me.

"*I bear testimony that you cannot sink farther than the light and sweeping intelligence of Jesus Christ can reach. I bear testimony that as long as there is one spark of the will to repent and to reach,* he is there. *He did not just descend* to *your condition; he descended* below *it,* 'that he might be in all and through all things, the light of truth (D&C 88:6).'"[11]

President Thomas S. Monson tells the story of Clinton Duffy, a warden at San Quentin Prison who understood that

men can change. He relates, "A critic who knew of Warden Duffy's efforts to rehabilitate [inmates] said, 'Don't you know that leopards can't change their spots?'

"Warden Duffy responded, 'You should know I don't work with leopards. I work with men, and men change every day.'"[12]

We have the inspiring scriptural examples of change in the stories of Alma and the sons of Mosiah who, before their conversion and repentance, were the "very vilest of sinners" (Mosiah 28:4) and the Apostle Paul, who said he had once been the chief of sinners (see 1 Timothy 1:15).

Like these great men, we can also find the courage and strength to change the direction of our lives. I would like to share the example of someone very close to me who did change. My dear friend was born into a strong Latter-day Saint family, but in her teens stopped attending church. At one point along the way, she lost her membership. As the years went by, we, her family and close friends, never gave up on her. In time, like Enos, the teachings of her childhood that had "sunk deep into [her] heart" (Enos 1:3) came back to her remembrance, and she desired to come back into full church fellowship. She was ready for baptism except for one problem—she could not give up smoking. She had tried everything—nicotine patches, giving up slowly, going cold turkey—but nothing worked. My friend just did not have the strength to do it! Her very wise and loving bishop suggested that she read the Book of Mormon, which she had never done before. She took up the challenge and started reading. As she read and prayed mightily, her faith in God and Christ increased; she came to understand the doctrine of the Atonement and what it meant in her life. She read the beautiful story of Alma and, no doubt, learned of the "exquisite and sweet" joy (Alma 36:21) that came into his life after repentance. With the increased understanding and vision that came to her as she read the Book of Mormon, she gained the spiritual strength to live the Word of Wisdom. In time, we saw a visible change come over her—she just glowed with joy! Her entire demeanor was altered as the light of the gospel came into her life. We truly saw that she had "experienced this mighty change" of heart that Alma talks about (Alma 5:14).

Her only sorrow was that she had not changed the direction of her life sooner and worried about her family and the consequences of years of inactivity. She would have been comforted by these words from Elder Jeffrey R. Holland, "God doesn't care nearly as much about where you have been as He does about where you are and, with His help, where you are willing to go."[13]

Elder Neil L. Andersen explained, "Repentance not only changes us, but it also blesses our families and those we love. With our righteous repentance, in the timetable of the Lord, the lengthened-out arms of the Savior will not only encircle us but will also extend into the lives of our children and posterity. Repentance always means that there is greater happiness ahead."[14]

My friend was soon rebaptized and gained a peace and joy that she had not felt in many years.

You might be familiar with the inspiring story of Al Fox Carraway, a convert to the church, who has spoken and written about change. Reflecting upon her life, she said, "Don't let who you used to be stop you from who you can become."[15]

I love the painting by Carl Bloch of the Savior with his arms outstretched in love to all. It can remind us that repentance is for each of us—both young or old, rich or poor, for our mistakes both big and small. Elder Neil L. Andersen has said, "For most, repenting is quiet and quite private, daily seeking the Lord's help to make needed changes."[16] And with His help, each day we can be a little bit more like Him. The Savior is always there, ready and waiting to extend to us all the blessings of repentance—if we just come unto Him.

To me, it seems appropriate that there is a child in the Carl Bloch painting, as the Lord has instructed us in the Doctrine and Covenants that we should teach our children the doctrine of repentance (see D&C 68:25). Likewise, in the Book of Mormon we are taught, "We talk of Christ, we rejoice in Christ, we preach of Christ, we prophesy of Christ, . . . that our children may know to what source they may look for a remission of their sins" (2 Nephi 25:26).

How blessed we are to have this knowledge of Christ's Atonement!

Years ago, our high school–aged son and two other young priests were administering the sacrament. As they turned back the white cloth, we saw a look of shock on their faces—there was no bread! Hoping that he could find a leftover loaf, our son slipped into the preparation room—but there was none to be found. Finally, our worried son quietly walked over to the bishop and explained the problem. That very wise bishop then stood up, shared the situation with the congregation, and then asked a very insightful question, "How would it be if the sacrament table were empty today because there had been no Atonement of Jesus Christ?" My husband and I have thought of that often—what if there was no bread because there was no crucifixion; no water because there was no shedding of blood?

I am so grateful that there is an Atonement and for the blessings it brings. As we strive daily to "change the direction of our sails" and become more like Christ, I testify that hope, peace, and healing will come into our lives.

Repentance:
The Pathway to Perfection

Tad R. Callister

Suppose for a moment someone said to you: "I just wrote a book and I would like you to peruse it." What would that mean to you? To many the word *peruse* means to casually review or skim over, but its historical or traditional meaning is exactly the opposite. The Oxford Dictionary explains as follows: "Note that peruse means 'read' . . . with . . . thoroughness and care. It does not mean 'read through quickly; [or to] glance over.'"[1]

The word *repentance* faces a somewhat similar challenge. It too is often misused and misunderstood. Some, hearing the word *repentance*, immediately think of sin and hellfire and damnation. To them it is a negative, but to the contrary, repentance is a glorious positive; it is but another name for the process that perfects us. So glorious is this principle that John and Peter Whitmer were both told by the Lord "that the thing which will be of the most worth unto you will be to declare repentance unto this people" (D&C 15:6; 16:6). Simply put, repentance is the key that unlocks the powers of the Savior's Atonement that can both cleanse us and perfect us.

84

In order to properly discuss the relationship between the Atonement and repentance I would like to begin by raising two critical questions: First, why is the Atonement necessary, and second, why is repentance necessary? First, the Atonement:

Some time ago I met with a group of Muslims. They were good men. It wasn't long, however, before they asked the inevitable question: "Why is the Atonement of Jesus Christ necessary? Why can't God, who is all powerful, just forgive us when we repent or help us overcome our weaknesses without the sacrifice of His Son?" Suppose for a moment a man, contemplating an exhilarating freefall, makes a rash decision and spontaneously jumps from a plane. After doing so, he quickly realizes the foolishness of his actions. He wants to land safely, but there is an obstacle—the law of gravity. He moves his arms with astounding speed, hoping to fly, but to no avail. He positions his body to float or glide so as to slow the descent, but the law of gravity is unrelenting and unmerciful. He tries to reason with this basic law of nature: "It was a mistake. I will never do it again. I have learned my lesson." But his pleas and petitions fall on deaf ears. The law of gravity, like the law of justice, has no passion; it knows no mercy; it has no forgiveness; and it knows no exceptions. Fortuitously though, he suddenly feels something on his back. A friend in the plane, sensing his moment of foolishness, had placed a parachute there just before the jump. He finds the rip cord and pulls it. Relieved, he floats safely to the ground. Now, we might ask: "Was the law of gravity violated or compromised in any way? Or rather, was another law invoked that was compatible yet merciful?"

When we sin we are like the foolish man who jumped from the plane. No matter what we do on our own, only a crash

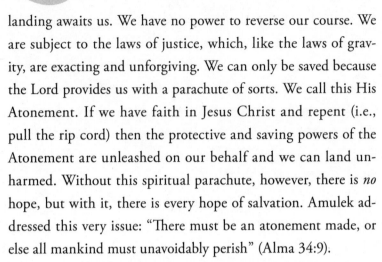

landing awaits us. We have no power to reverse our course. We are subject to the laws of justice, which, like the laws of gravity, are exacting and unforgiving. We can only be saved because the Lord provides us with a parachute of sorts. We call this His Atonement. If we have faith in Jesus Christ and repent (i.e., pull the rip cord) then the protective and saving powers of the Atonement are unleashed on our behalf and we can land unharmed. Without this spiritual parachute, however, there is *no* hope, but with it, there is every hope of salvation. Amulek addressed this very issue: "There must be an atonement made, or else all mankind must unavoidably perish" (Alma 34:9).

I do not know if there is some external law of justice independent of God to which He is subject or if God determines the laws of justice to which all beings in the universe including Himself must be governed, or a combination of the two. What I do know, and the scriptures confirm, is that a law of justice exists and no fallen man can be saved without the Atonement of Jesus Christ on one hand and repentance on the other. They are inseparable partners in the saving process.

Recognizing that the Atonement is necessary, some might ask next: "But *why* is repentance necessary?" Why can't we just suffer for our sins and, when the price is paid, go to heaven on a delayed schedule? In other words, does paying the full price of our sins on our own have the same consequence as repenting of our sins with the aid of the Atonement? The answer is a resounding no! You recall that Nephi addressed this topic. He said, "There shall be many which shall say: Eat, drink, and be merry, for tomorrow we die; and . . . if it so be that we are guilty, God will beat us with a few stripes, and at last we shall be saved in the kingdom of God" (2 Nephi 28:7–8). And then Nephi shared with us God's feelings about this ideology: "Yea, and there shall be many which shall teach after this manner, false and vain and foolish doctrines" (2 Nephi 28:9). Perhaps the following chart best illustrates the consequences of the self-payment program on one hand versus repentance on the other:

	Self-payment	Repentance and the Atonement
Pain	Incredible	Substantial, but Christ picks up much
Meets demands of justice	Yes	Yes
Cleanses us	No	Yes
Removes guilt	No	Yes
Changes us	No	Yes
Perfects us	No	Yes
Exalts us	No	Yes

If we were to pay the full price of our sins on our own, the pain would be incredible. The Doctrine and Covenants explains, "But if they would not repent they must suffer even as I; which suffering caused myself, even God, the greatest of all, to tremble because of pain" (D&C 19:17–18). Would our suffering meet the demands of justice? Yes, because the scriptures declare: "None shall be exempted from the justice and the laws of God" (D&C 107:84). Would it cleanse us? No, for the scriptures tell us that only the "blood of Jesus Christ his Son cleanseth us from all sin" (1 John 1:7). Can self-payment remove the guilt? No. If it cannot cleanse us of sin, it certainly cannot remove the associated guilt. Will it change us? No. Suppose two men committed the same crime. Does the man who serves his full ten-year sentence in prison emerge having changed to the same degree as the man who is released after five years for good behavior? Justice can only exact punishment—it is an external force that has no power in and of itself to change the inward man.

While serving as a mission president, I encountered a young missionary who was struggling with obedience. I met with him multiple times. Finally at one of these counseling sessions he blurted out:

"What do you want me to do?"

I replied, "I'm sorry, but you've missed the point. It's not what *I* want you to do that matters; it should be *what do you want to do.*"

There was a moment of silence, and then I think he made the most thoughtful statement I heard on my entire mission: "President," he said, "*you don't want me just to change my behavior, you want me to change my nature.*"

"Yes," I nodded, "you have it." If he only changed his behavior, if he only got up on time because his companion leaned on him to do so, if he was only obedient because his companion was present and insisted on it, then he would go home and be the same person he was before he left, subject to the same weaknesses and temptations. But if with the Lord's help he changed his nature and he got up every morning on time whether or not someone told him to; if he was obedient whether or not someone was looking, then his nature would have changed and when he went home he would be a much different young man than the one who entered the mission field. He would have a new resolve and strength to combat the temptations to which he had previously yielded. He would have the power to conquer his old Goliaths. Justice may mandate a change in our behavior, but only through repentance can the way be opened for the Atonement to change our nature (see Mosiah 5:2).

Will compliance with justice perfect us? No. If self-payment cannot change us, it certainly cannot perfect us. Can our own suffering exalt us? No. The scriptures declare: "All men, everywhere must repent, or they can in nowise inherit the kingdom of God, for no unclean thing can dwell there" (Moses 6:57).

Now on the other hand, what if we were to avail ourselves of the Savior's Atonement by repenting, what difference would it make in the consequences? The pain would be substantial, but much less than the full pain because Christ pays for a portion of it. Would the Atonement satisfy justice? Yes. Amulek taught, "And thus mercy can satisfy the demands of justice, and encircles them in the arms of safety, while he that exercises no faith unto repentance is exposed to the whole law of the demands of justice" (Alma 34:16). Can repentance cleanse us? Yes, through the blood and Atonement of Christ. Remove our guilt? Yes, as we will discuss in greater detail. Change us? Yes. Elder Dallin H. Oaks observed: "The repenting sinner must suffer for his sins, but this suffering has a different purpose than punishment or payment. Its purpose is *change*."[2] Does it perfect us? Yes. Moroni declared: "By his grace ye may be perfect in Christ" (Moroni 10:32). Does the Atonement exalt us? Yes. Nephi explains that there is no way other than through Christ that we can be saved (see 2 Nephi 31:21). Sometimes we forget that repentance is not only the road to forgiveness; it is also the road to perfection.

Suppose I invited one of you who live out of state to drive to our home in Bountiful, but I asked you to drive there in neutral.

You might respond, "That's impossible—I can't."

I might reply, "Just push the pedal to the metal."

Frustrated, you might answer, "But I can't get there unless I put my car in gear." So it is with our spiritual progress—we can't get to our desired destination in neutral—we must put our spirit in gear. That is called repentance.

In this regard, President David O. McKay further said, "'Every principle and ordinance of the gospel of Jesus Christ is significant and important . . . but there is none more essential to the salvation of the human family than the divine and eternally operative principle, repentance. *Without it, no one can be saved. Without it, no one can even progress.*'"[3]

When all is said and done, we can either choose the self-payment program that is devoid of hope or happiness, or accept the Savior's Atonement through repentance that entitles us to glorious blessings and unlimited hope. It seems like such an easy choice—incredible pain and unhappiness on one hand or less pain and unbelievable happiness on the other.

When we sin, we feel embarrassed, discouraged, unclean, and estranged from God's spirit. We lose self-confidence and thus often lose hope in ourselves and the future. Sometimes we even give up. King Benjamin taught that truth in no uncertain terms: "If [a] man repenteth not . . . the demands of divine justice do awaken his immortal soul to a lively sense of his own guilt . . . and doth fill his breast with guilt, and pain, and anguish" (Mosiah 2:38; see also Alma 42:18). This same truth was also taught by President Ezra Taft Benson: "You can't *do* wrong and *feel* right."[4]

Because we are God's children and because He loves us, His plan called for Jesus Christ to pay the price to bring about a condition that can eventually reverse all the negative feelings of sin and replace them with peace and hope and self-confidence. This condition is called repentance.

On occasion, while serving as a church leader, I met with good members whom I believed had repented, but who confessed they still lived with troubled consciences. This struck me forcibly when speaking with a convert to our Church of about fifteen years. He had been faithful and devoted from the day of his baptism, but wondered if the Lord could possibly forgive him for his checkered life before he accepted the gospel message. It just seemed too much to ask. Some people have innocently, but *incorrectly*, placed limits on the Savior's redemptive powers. They have converted His *infinite* Atonement to a *finite* one that somehow falls short of their particular sin. But it is an infinite Atonement, because it encompasses and circumscribes every sin, every weakness, every addiction, every wrong, and every finite frailty of man.

Once we have repented there is no black mark on our right ankle that reads "2010 mistake," no stain behind our left ear that says "2015 transgression." There is no such thing as a spotted or crème-colored repenter in God's kingdom. Rather it is as Isaiah said, "Though your sins be as scarlet, *they shall be as white as snow*" (Isaiah 1:18; emphasis added) or as Moroni said, "Ye become holy, without spot" (Moroni 10:33). The Atonement leaves no clues, no evidence of any past sin. It wipes the slate completely clean. That is the miracle and gift of the Atonement of Jesus Christ.

Even though we may believe in His Atonement, the question often arises: How do I know if I have been forgiven of my sins?

The Doctrine and Covenants gives one test: "By this ye may know if a man repenteth of his sins—behold, he will confess them and forsake them" (D&C 58:43). But I believe there is also another test. If we feel the Spirit in our life when we pray or read the scriptures, or teach or testify, or at any other time, then that is our witness that we have been forgiven or, alternatively, that the cleansing process is taking place—for the Spirit cannot dwell in an unclean vessel (see Alma 7:21; see also Helaman 4:24). In most cases the cleansing process takes time because our change in nature takes time, but in the interim, we can proceed with the confidence that God approves of our progress to a sufficient degree that we can enjoy some measure of His Spirit.[5]

Some have asked: But if I am forgiven, why do I still feel guilty? Perhaps in God's mercy the memory of that guilt is a warning, a spiritual stop sign of sorts that cries out when similar temptations confront us: "Don't go down that road. You know the pain it can bring." Perhaps for those in the process of repenting, it is meant to be a protection, not a punishment.

Will our guilt ever go away? The promise of the Lord is certain in that regard. To the repentant the Lord promised that the time would come when *"their joy shall be full forever"* (2 Nephi 9:18; emphasis added), meaning there will come a time when there will be no past twinges or pangs of guilt. The scriptures further confirm this truth: "And God shall wipe away all tears from their eyes; and there shall be no more . . . sorrow, nor crying, *neither shall there be any more pain: for the former things are passed away*" (Revelation 21:4; emphasis added), meaning they are gone. While our Lord's Atonement does not wipe away the past, in some miraculous way it has the power to wipe away all the sorrow and pain associated with the past. Perhaps it is like the experience of breaking a bone. When it completely heals we can still remember the event that triggered the break, but the pain is gone. Christ is the great physician who has that healing power.

I do not know if we will ever forget our sins, but the consequence will be the same as if we did, for the time will come when the repentant will no longer be troubled by their sins. Such was the case with the Book of Mormon prophets Enos and Alma, each of whom sought a remission of past sins. As to Enos, the scriptures record: "And there came a voice unto me, saying: Enos, thy sins are forgiven thee . . . *wherefore, my guilt was swept away.* And I said: Lord, how is it done? And he said unto me: *Because of thy faith in Christ*" (Enos 1:5–8; emphasis added). Enos had faith that Christ's Atonement could not only cleanse his sins but also remove his guilt. Alma, while reflecting upon the Atonement and his sinful past, exclaimed: "While I was harrowed up by the memory of my many sins, behold, . . . I cried within my heart: O Jesus, thou Son of God, have mercy on me. . . . *And now, behold, when I thought this,* I could *remember my pains no more; yea, I was harrowed up by the memory of my sins no more*" (Alma 36:17–19; emphasis added). So complete was this healing process that Alma then adds, "There can be nothing so exquisite and sweet as was my joy" (Alma 36:21). Alma didn't forget his sins; in fact, he was recalling them at that precise moment, but somehow the miracle of the Atonement was so expansive, so penetrating that it removed not just part but *all* of his guilt associated with those wrongful deeds.

Whatever our status in life, we can be comforted by the truth that God will ultimately judge us by what we become, not by what we were. That was Scrooge's realization in Dickens's *A Christmas Carol*. He had so transformed his life that he could now rightfully declare, "I am not the man I was."[6] And that is the truth taught by the Apostle Paul, "Therefore if any man be in Christ [meaning he repents], *he is a new creature*: old things are passed away; behold, all things are become new" (2 Corinthians 5:17; see also Mosiah 27:25–26). For the repentant, the guilt will pass away because with perfect honesty they can each say, I am not the person who committed that sin; I am born again; I am a new creature in Jesus Christ.

President Joseph Fielding Smith shared the story of a woman who had repented of her immoral conduct but was still struggling with feelings of guilt. She asked him what she should do now. In turn, he asked her to read to him the account of Sodom and Gomorrah—of Lot and of Lot's wife, who was turned to a pillar of salt because she looked back after being told not to do so (see Genesis 19:26). Then he asked the woman what lessons those verses held for her. She answered, "The Lord will destroy those who are wicked."

"Not so," replied President Smith. "The lesson for *you* is 'Don't look back!'"[7] Such is also the lesson for each of us.

In this regard Paul, who called himself the "chief of sinners" (see 1 Timothy 1:15), counseled us as follows: "Brethren, I count not myself to have apprehended [meaning to have become like God]: but this one thing I do, *forgetting those things which are behind*, and reaching forth unto those things which are before, I press toward the mark for the prize of the high calling of God in Christ Jesus" (Philippians 3:13–14; emphasis added). In other words, if we place our faith in Jesus Christ then we can proceed forward with that glorious assurance that Christ has descended not only beneath our sins, *but also our guilt,* and thereby one day we can be free of both (see Mosiah 5:8). Then we will be at perfect peace with God and with ourselves.

But repentance is not just overcoming our sins; it is also an active pursuit to acquire Godlike traits. It is a humble recognition of the distance between us and God, and a compelling desire to narrow the gap. It is a fresh perspective that we can, with the aid of the Atonement, arise above our mortal weaknesses and limitations and become like God, our Father.

But how does the Savior's Atonement work to overcome our weaknesses and ultimately perfect us? Perhaps the underlying reasoning goes something like this: Through the ordinance of baptism we are cleansed because of the Atonement of Jesus Christ. As a result of that cleansing, we are eligible to receive the gift of the Holy Ghost. With the gift of the Holy Ghost comes the right to receive the gifts of the Spirit. Each of the gifts of the Spirit (e.g., faith, love, wisdom, patience, and so on) represents an attribute of godliness; therefore as we acquire the gifts of the Spirit we acquire the attributes of godliness.

Elder George Q. Cannon, an apostle, spoke of man's shortcomings and the divine solution to perfection. Recognizing the link between grace, gifts, and godhood, he fervently pled with the members of the Church to overcome each personal weakness through the acquisition of a countermanding gift of strength known as the gift of the Spirit. He said:

"No man ought to say, 'Oh, I cannot help this; it is my nature.' He is not justified in it, for the reason that God has promised to give strength to correct these things, and to give gifts that will eradicate them."[8] He also said, *"If any of us are imperfect, it is our duty to pray for the gift that will make us perfect."*[9]

We can pray for gifts of the Spirit, made possible by Christ's Atonement, which will lift us above our mortal weaknesses and further our pursuit of godhood. As we pray and seek after these gifts we are engaging in the act of repentance; we are progressing towards Godhood—we are putting off the old man and giving birth to a new one.

But oh, what a cost to make this possible. It cost the life and blood and suffering of the holiest man this Earth has even known. Some have contended His suffering was not real, not akin to man's suffering, because He was half divine and therefore had a divine shield to protect Him against the vicissitudes of life. In order to teach the correct principle, my wife and I, who jointly taught seminary, invited one of the young men in our class to come forward. We took a marker and drew a line down the center of his face. We then gave him a shield to hold in his right hand. We then asked the class to imagine that the right side of him was divine, while the other side was mortal. We then invited a young lady to come forth and gave her four paper balls wrapped in tape. The first one was labeled "death."

We said, "Throw it at him as hard as you can." With delight, she did so, but the young man raised his shield and blocked it. She then threw the second ball, labeled "sin," the third, labeled "weaknesses," and the fourth, labeled "common ailments of life." Each time, the young man blocked the ball with his shield, demonstrating that the Savior did have the divine power to protect Himself against these mortal obstacles, if He so chose, but of course He did not. Next, we instructed the young woman to repeat the process, but this time the young man was instructed not to raise his shield, even though he had it. With even greater delight the young lady threw each of the four balls and hit him each time.

While the Savior did have a divine shield, He never raised it to protect Himself or immunize Himself in any way against the afflictions of mortality; rather, He used His divinity only to enlarge the cup of wrath He would suffer. How so? Each of us has within us a release valve. When our pain becomes so exquisite this release valve "kicks in" and we either become unconscious or we die, but the Savior used His divinity to keep the release valve open until He had suffered the pain of all men and women of all ages of all worlds. This truth was confirmed by King Benjamin, who declared that Christ suffered "even more than man can suffer" (Mosiah 3:7; see also Hebrews 2:9; 14–18).

With this knowledge of His Atonement we can forge ahead in life with good cheer whatever the challenges or obstacles may be. In the most difficult week of the Savior's life He could nonetheless give us this hope: "In the world ye shall have tribulation: but be of good cheer; I have overcome the world" (John 16:33). Because of the Atonement there is no external event, no outside circumstance, be it death, disaster, or the like that can rob us of our exaltation if we but repent. We are in the driver's seat as to our divine destiny.

I bear my solemn witness that Jesus Christ is indeed all He claimed to be—the Savior and Redeemer of the World. I bear testimony that if we repent and avail ourselves of His Atonement, He can cleanse us, console us, and ultimately perfect us.

The Small but Important Things

Peggy S. Worthen

I would like to begin by sharing the parable of the caramel apples. There were two young sisters. One Saturday morning their mother gave the two sisters a task. The mother had bought a large bag of apples and several bags of wrapped caramels, and she desired that her two young daughters make caramel apples. It didn't matter to her when they made them, as long as the task was completed before their bedtime that night.

The young sisters had helped their mother make caramel apples before, so the mother and her daughters were confident that they could do this task without her help. Well, the young sisters waited until it was about bedtime to begin making the caramel apples. They were confident that it would only take them a little while.

However, they soon realized that they were mistaken. First of all, it took a very long time to unwrap all of the caramels. Then, after putting the caramels into a double boiler, it took a very long time for them to melt, and they were not melting as they should. The result was a potful of thick, pasty caramel.

The sisters tried dipping the apples into the caramel as they had seen their mother do, but the caramel was not sticking to the apples as it had when their mother had dipped apples. The two sisters soon realized that there was no way that the pasty caramel was going to stick easily to the apples. The only way they could make the caramel stick was by spooning up globs of the caramel paste and applying it with the spoon onto the apple, sometimes using their fingers to get the caramel off the spoon and onto the apples.

One of the problems they faced was that as soon as the caramel was out of the warm pot it quickly began to cool, making matters worse. What a mess! Instead of looking like the beautiful caramel apples with the smooth creamy finish that they had helped their mother make, their caramel apples were lumpy and uneven.

The younger sister was becoming tired and miserable. She felt terrible. She just wanted to go to bed and forget about this caramel-apple business. She wanted to cry—and probably did—but tears or no, she knew that they had to finish. And it seemed like it would take forever. She believed the caramel apple nightmare would never end. But finally, and to her great relief, they were finished and were able to go to bed.

The next morning their mother saw all of the lumpy-looking caramel apples. She commented on how long it must have taken them to complete. She thanked her daughters and then said, "You know, I believe it would have been a great deal easier for you if you had added water to the caramels." And the sisters were amazed. It was such a seemingly minor detail, but a very important detail indeed.

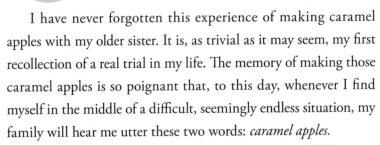

I have never forgotten this experience of making caramel apples with my older sister. It is, as trivial as it may seem, my first recollection of a real trial in my life. The memory of making those caramel apples is so poignant that, to this day, whenever I find myself in the middle of a difficult, seemingly endless situation, my family will hear me utter these two words: *caramel apples*.

This experience, like a parable, is a nice story. And, like a parable, over the years it has taken on a much broader, deeper meaning for me. In fact, the experience has taught me several important lessons. From this experience I learned that no matter how difficult and trying an experience may be—even if it may be a lifelong challenge—we can still be happy and have joy. I also learned that while we are going through those difficult times, if we pay careful attention we will notice the tender mercies from our Heavenly Father. For example, in the case of my dreadful caramel-apple experience, even though I was tired and miserable, I did, after all, have all the delicious caramels I could possibly want to eat.

But the most important lesson I learned is that we should never forget to do the small and simple things. If we had remembered to add two tablespoons of water to the caramels—a very small but important ingredient in the caramel-apple recipe—the caramel would have easily adhered to the apples and the entire situation would have been much better. Similarly, in our challenging life experiences, if we will do the simple but important things such as daily scripture study, daily prayer, and regular service, our lives will be better.

In my mind the water in the parable is a lot like covenants in our lives. They may seem simple and routine and we may sometimes overlook the need for them, but they are the things that hold everything else together in trying times. Without covenants, things fall apart—just as the caramel did without the water. With covenants, things come together, in large part because covenants connect us to Heavenly Father, the One who can make "all things work together for [our] good" (Romans 8:28). Covenants truly connect us to God and to the powers of heaven. This knowledge has brought great comfort and peace to me.

I recently asked a friend what she thought it meant to be connected to Heavenly Father through making and keeping covenants. She immediately thought of Matthew 11:28–30, which says: "Come unto me, all ye that labour and are heavy laden, and I will give you rest. Take my yoke upon you, and learn of me . . . : and ye shall find rest unto your souls. For my yoke is easy, and my burden is light."

When we make covenants with our Heavenly Father, we become connected to Him through allowing Him to help us by taking His yoke upon us. When we are connected—or yoked—to Him, He is able to make our burdens lighter because we are not relying solely on our own power but on His infinite power as well.

My friend pointed out that when we connect ourselves with Heavenly Father by making covenants with Him, we form a partnership with Him. When we are keeping our covenants, we are able to receive personal revelation from Him as our partner. Many times through personal revelation we are guided to help other people. We are guided to serve. Heavenly Father will call on us through the Holy Ghost to carry out His purposes in ways that also bless our lives.

My friend related an experience that she had in which she was inspired or guided to help another person. She shared this

experience in a letter to one of her children who was at the time serving a mission. She wrote:

"The highlight of my week . . . was a spontaneous visit to [a neighbor] who is not doing too well physically. On my busiest day of the week, as I was jotting down all of the things I needed to do, I thought I ought to visit her. So I wrote it down on my list, but in prioritizing tasks, I recognized that I would have to visit her at another time.

"[Later that day], as I was delivering fliers [on] her street [for an upcoming neighborhood event], I had the thought come to mind again to visit [my neighbor]. I decided to be brave and to just act on my thought. So I [hesitatingly] knocked on her door. [I felt a little awkward coming by unannounced without anything to offer. Her husband answered the door. I] was invited in and found that my visit was the very thing she needed in that moment. She was feeling incredibly discouraged. She was lying down on a little cot close to the floor and could hardly move. She had tears come to her eyes as she told me how much she needed my visit that day. We visited for just a short time, but as I left, I felt thankful for and a bit in awe at the promptings I had received that led me to her. It was a witness of a loving Heavenly Father who is acutely aware of the needs of each of His children. In that moment I felt in a small way that I had been His hands and voice to [my neighbor]. I am thankful for that experience and hope to be in tune enough with the Spirit to never miss an opportunity to be on God's errand."

As a result of that experience, my friend felt a connection to Heavenly Father; she felt a partnership with Him. Through her willingness to act upon a prompting from the Holy Ghost, my friend was able to help another person feel Heavenly Father's love, and she felt His love for her as well.

My friend expressed the happiness that she felt as a result of this experience. She was reminded of what a blessing it is to be able to serve, and she also felt a real connection to Heavenly Father.

Not only can we feel the blessing of happiness through covenant keeping, we can also feel and experience the power associated with it. Doctrine and Covenants 82:10 states, "I, the Lord, am bound when ye do what I say." He promises to help us, and that is powerful help.

The knowledge that keeping our covenants brings us happiness and that we have His promise to help us throughout our lives increases my desire to keep the covenants I have made. This does not, however, exempt us from challenges, but it is comforting to know that our burdens will be made easier because we are yoked to Him. He promises us that.

As I think about the ways in which I can better enable myself to keep covenants, I think about athletes and musicians. You may wonder what these two groups of people have to do with covenant keeping and the blessings and power that come from covenant keeping; I will explain.

I enjoy watching athletic events. I also enjoy listening to beautiful music. Because I am not an athlete or a musician, I probably do not fully appreciate the efforts of those who perform, but I do know that before any performance there is a lot of work that goes on behind the scenes. For example, athletes spend hour after hour, day after day, going through grueling workouts. They lift weights, they do push-ups, they do pull-ups, and they do sit-ups. They run

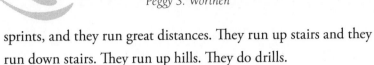

sprints, and they run great distances. They run up stairs and they run down stairs. They run up hills. They do drills.

I asked my daughter, who played basketball on her high school team several years ago, what part of practice was the most difficult for her. She said it was the ladder drill that they performed on the football field. I asked her what this drill consisted of. You may already know, but for you who do not, I will explain. The athletes start on the goal line, run as fast as they can to the five-yard line, and then run back to the goal line as fast as they can. Then they run as fast as they can to the ten-yard line and then back to the goal line as fast as they can. Then they run as fast as they can to the twenty-yard line and then back as fast as they can to the goal line. (I am getting a workout just explaining this to you!) This drill goes on and on until they have reached the goal line on the other side of the field—100 yards away. Sounds like great fun!

I recently asked a former football player what part of practice was the most difficult for him. He told me that it was conditioning. Again, you may already know what this is, but just in case you do not, I will explain. Conditioning is the part of the practice that follows the structured practice. He described it as when you "empty your tank"; you expend any energy you may have left. This is the time when you run wind sprints. I looked up *wind sprint* in the dictionary. It is described as "a sprint performed as a training exercise to develop breathing capacity especially during exertion."[1] In other words, you work as hard as you can until you have no energy left. What is the purpose of this? It is to make you stronger and better.

Musicians also spend hour after hour, day after day, going through their own grueling practices. I asked a friend who is an accomplished pianist what part of practicing is the most difficult for her. She said it is staying focused. What she meant is that when you are practicing a piece of music, you have to practice it correctly, and playing a piece of music correctly every time can be a slow and tedious process. You have to think hard and try hard. She said it is mentally exerting. And sometimes it is very difficult to think and stay focused. The purpose of all the tedious and mentally exerting practice is to ensure that when it is time to perform, the performance will be perfectly executed.

I asked my daughter, the former football player, and the accomplished pianist what it was that made them keep coming back time after time for ever more difficult practicing. They each gave me a similar response. Surprisingly, it wasn't just that they knew that this strenuous effort would pay off at performance time. The bottom line was that being able to accomplish these difficult things made them happy, even before the performance. They pushed themselves to the limit in part because the very striving brought them happiness.

I am not an athlete or an accomplished musician, but in a small way I understand what they mean. I have done strenuous exercise and I have had the opportunity of tackling a difficult piano piece. I have felt the joy and sense of accomplishment that comes from hard work—and that makes me happy.

When we exercise or exert ourselves mentally, our bodies release chemicals called endorphins. Endorphins produce an increased sense of well-being and are described as having a "much greater analgesic potency than morphine."[2] In other words, endorphins make you feel good—they make you happy. Feeling the effects of endorphins may be one of the reasons that athletes

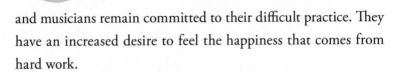
and musicians remain committed to their difficult practice. They have an increased desire to feel the happiness that comes from hard work.

If doing difficult physical and mental things gives us the benefits of physical endorphins, then perhaps exercising our faith and keeping our covenants may help us experience the benefits of what I would call "spiritual endorphins." Elder Richard G. Scott reminded us: "We were taught in the premortal world that our purpose in coming here is to be tested, tried, and stretched. . . . Despite all of the negative challenges we have in life, we must take time to actively exercise our faith. Such exercise invites the positive, faith-filled power of the Atonement of Jesus Christ into our lives."[3]

As we continually exercise our faith and keep our covenants, we can experience joy—we can experience the benefits of "spiritual endorphins"—even in the times of stress and striving. Thus, keeping our covenants helps us through both the daily conditioning and the more dramatic challenges that we confront.

The more we experience the blessings and power that come through exercising our faith and keeping our covenants, the more our desire will increase to make and keep sacred covenants. I am grateful for the blessings of covenants. I know that covenants connect us to our Heavenly Father and to the powers of heaven. I know that as we keep our covenants and exercise our faith, Heavenly Father will guide us to carry out His purposes—blessing not only our lives, but the lives of others. As we connect ourselves to Heavenly Father through covenant keeping, He will make our burdens lighter and we will experience the happiness and joy that He desires for us.

Covenants Connect Us to Heaven

Kevin J Worthen

One of the most remarkable episodes in recorded history is found in Alma 24. It involves the experience of thousands of Lamanites who were converted to the gospel of Jesus Christ by Ammon and his brethren in the century prior to the birth of the Savior. Shortly after their conversion, these good Saints, who became known as the people of Ammon, faced a momentous challenge, one as dramatic as could be imagined. Some of their fellow countrymen who had not accepted the gospel had begun "to make preparations for war against" them (v. 4). And they were planning a lot more than a verbal assault on the ideology or good name of these recent converts. They literally "took up arms" against the people of Ammon with the intent "to destroy their brethren" (vv. 2, 5).

Facing this daunting prospect, the leaders of this group decided to "hold a council" to determine "what they should do to defend themselves against" the impending attack (v. 5). The course they chose was most unusual. "Not one soul" of them was willing to "take up arms against their brethren," nor would they "even make any preparations for war" (v. 6). This was not because they lacked the weapons or the expertise to defend themselves in such a manner. Prior to their conversion they were described as a people "whose hearts delight[ed] in the shedding of blood" (Alma 26:24).

But rather than relying on conventional weapons and tactics, these faithful Saints determined to trust in the power of covenants with God. Instead of taking up their swords, they resolved to lay them aside, "covenanting with God, that rather than shed the blood of their brethren they would give up their own lives" (Alma 24:18), secure in the belief that "if our brethren destroy us, behold, we shall go to our God and shall be saved" (v. 16).

Acting on this resolve, they buried their weapons of war "deep in the earth" (v. 16). And when their attackers arrived on the battle scene determined to conquer them, these covenant people of God "went out to meet them, and prostrated themselves before them to the earth, and began to call on the name of the Lord; and thus they were in this attitude when the Lamanites began to fall upon them, and began to slay them with the sword" (v. 21).

The immediate temporal result was the slaughter of more than a thousand of those faithful, innocent Saints (see v. 22). But the more important, more eternal results soon became apparent. As it began to dawn on many of the attackers what was happening, their hearts were immediately changed, and "they threw down their weapons of war . . . ; and they came down even as their brethren, relying upon the mercies of those whose arms were lifted to slay them" (v. 25).

The Book of Mormon records the eventual outcome: "And

it came to pass that the people of God were joined that day by more than the number who had been slain; and those who had been slain were righteous people, therefore we have no reason to doubt but what they were saved" (v. 26).

There is perhaps no written account that more vividly illustrates the eternal power and impact of covenants or that more impressively reminds us that such power will often come as the result of sacrifice—*real* sacrifice that is much more than symbolic or superficial.

The particular covenant that the people of Ammon entered into with God was unique to them and to their distinctive situation. But the overarching principle about the critical role that covenants play in the accomplishment of God's plans for His children is fully applicable to us today and, indeed, to all of God's children throughout the history of the world.

Covenants are central to God's plan for us. They were part of His plan from the outset. "The Prophet Joseph Smith taught that even before the organization of this earth, covenants were made in heaven."[1] In light of that long history, one might suppose that we will continue to make covenants in our next sphere of existence.

Given the centrality of covenants in God's plan, and with the vivid image fresh in our minds of the commitment to covenants demonstrated by the people of Ammon, I would like to address three simple questions:

1. What exactly are covenants?
2. How does covenant keeping make the powers of God more available to us?

3. How can we increase our desire and ability
to make and keep covenants in trying times?

These are basic questions. You may not learn or hear anything new from me, but I hope that you think about these questions in a different way.

WHAT ARE COVENANTS?

First, what are covenants? Well, I am a lawyer, so I will start
with a legal definition. According to *Black's Law Dictionary*, the
legal definition of a covenant is "an agreement . . . or promise of
two or more parties . . . by which either of the parties pledges
himself to the other that something is either done or shall be
done."[2] Wordy, I know—but that is what legal definitions are
like. Put a bit more simply, in the legal world, a covenant is a
mutual promise parties make to each other to do or refrain from
doing something. It is a contract.

In one respect this definition describes a covenant in the gospel sense as well. Gospel covenants are mutual promises made
between God and His children. In fact, Doctrine and Covenants
66:2 tells us that "the fulness of [the] gospel" is God's "everlasting covenant" with His children. As with legal covenants, this
everlasting covenant consists of mutual promises. In the most
general terms, God's promise is that He will give us all that He
has: eternal life. Our promise, on which His is dependent, is that
we will obey His commandments.

But there is one key difference between a covenant of law
and a gospel covenant. In the legal world, covenants are usually
the result of protracted negotiations—a matter of give-and-take

hammered out over time in a series of meetings. By contrast, as the Bible Dictionary notes, when a covenant is made between God and His children, "the two parties to the agreement do not stand in the relation of independent and equal contractors. God . . . fixes the terms, which man accepts."[3]

At first glance this difference would seem to turn the everlasting covenant between God and His children into what the law calls an adhesion contract—a take-it-or-leave-it offer imposed by a stronger party on a weaker party who has no realistic choice but to accept the unfair terms of the offer. In the legal world, adhesion contracts are often considered unconscionable, and therefore unenforceable, because they can be used to impose harsh conditions on people who, in the absence of coercion, would never agree to such unfair terms. Some—and I confess to having such feelings from time to time as a teenager—may view gospel covenants, and especially the commandments that are part of the everlasting covenant, as the harsh terms of a dictatorial parent imposed on His children merely as an arbitrary use of excessive power.

As with most things, however, the worldly view of the matter is inadequate to describe the things of God. God does not impose His covenants on any of His children. In fact, they are effective only if we accept them of our own free will and choice.

The fact that God determines the terms of the everlasting covenant without negotiating them with us is not an indication that He is trying to extract unfair promises from us. It is instead a reflection of two other more important differences between most legal covenants and gospel covenants.

One difference is that, unlike most people who enter into

legal contracts, God does not enter into covenants to gain something from the other party. Think about it: He already has eternal life. He already has all power, all knowledge, and all joy. The fact that He does not negotiate the terms of His covenants with us is not an indication that He wants to impose His will on us; instead it is a reminder of the reality that we really have nothing to give to Him because He already has it all. As King Benjamin reminded his people, if we would serve God with all our souls all our lives, we would still "be unprofitable servants" (Mosiah 2:21; see also vv. 20–24).

The gospel covenants may indeed be one-sided, but if so, it is God—and not us—who gets the short end of the bargain. God enters into everlasting covenants solely for our benefit—to help us lead the kind of life He leads, experience the kind of joy He experiences, and be the kind of being He is. The commandments He gives us are not negotiable because they are eternal laws that, as He has learned, must be obeyed if one is to experience true freedom, true joy, and true fulfillment.

This insight leads to the second key difference between a legal covenant or contract and a gospel covenant. Because parties who enter into legal contracts are generally motivated by self-interest, many contracting parties conclude that once it is clear that they have struck a bad bargain, the rational thing to do is breach the agreement, pay the damages to the other side, and walk away in search of a new and better bargain. And, in fact, in most situations, if the breaching parties are willing to make the other party whole (by paying damages), the law generally allows them to end the contract.[4] Thus legal contracts are by nature temporary and somewhat insecure.

By contrast, the covenants that God offers us are everlasting. As the Church handbook states, "A covenant is a sacred and *enduring* promise between God and His children."[5] Thus there is a level of commitment that God offers us that no earthly contracting party can offer. There is also a level of commitment He expects from us that is higher than earthly contract law demands.

In John 10:11–14, the Savior taught the difference between what Elder Bruce C. Hafen called the "contractual attitudes"[6] of the world and the covenant attitude of the Lord when He described the difference between the hireling and the good shepherd. As Elder Hafen noted, the hireling "performs his conditional promise of care only when he receives something in return."[7] Thus, "when the hireling 'seeth the wolf coming,' he 'leaveth the sheep, and fleeth . . . because he . . . careth not for the sheep.'"[8] The hireling has entered into a legal contract, not a gospel covenant. Motivated as he is by self-interest, when it is clear that what he is receiving in wages is not worth what he is being asked to do (which is to guard the sheep at the peril of his life), he calls off the contract. And under the earthly law, that is his right—as long as he is willing to pay the owner for the lost sheep.

By contrast, the Savior said, "I am the good shepherd" and "the good shepherd giveth his life for the sheep" (John 10:11). We can be sure that God will not walk away from His promises to us merely because He may have found a better bargain or have determined that circumstances have changed or that we are not worth the hassle. Unlike earthly legal promises, His covenant promises are eternal and enduring, operable "at all times and in all things, and in all places" (Mosiah 18:9).

In fact, to give us even greater assurance that His covenant promises are everlastingly secure, God often confirms those promises with an oath. For example, in Hebrews we read that "when God made promise to Abraham," He desired "more abundantly to shew unto the heirs of promise the immutability" (the unchangeable nature) of His promises, so He "confirmed" those promises "by an oath" (Hebrews 6:13, 17). And "because he could swear by no greater" (because there is nothing more certain than His godly character) "he sware by himself, saying, Surely blessing I will bless thee, and multiplying I will multiply thee" (Hebrews 6:13–14).[9] In other words, God was so serious about keeping His commitment to Abraham that He put His godhood on the line as a guarantee that He would keep His end of the bargain. That is an extraordinary guarantee—one that far supersedes any warranty that could possibly be given by mortals[10] and one that is available to all who are willing to enter into covenants with God.[11]

Understanding that God's covenants are selfless on His part and also eternal should motivate us to adhere to those covenants, even when it seemingly costs us a lot—even when, as in the case of the people of Ammon, it costs us our all. As Elder Hafen explained, contracting parties each agree to give 50 percent; covenant parties each agree to give 100 percent.[12] But in God's case, His 100 percent is infinitely larger than is ours. God has committed all that He has—including His Only Begotten Son—to enable Him to fulfill His end of the bargain. We should not then be surprised that He asks us to give all that we have (which is infinitely small in comparison) to make it work.

How Does Covenant Keeping Make the Powers of God More Available to Us?

How exactly does keeping covenants help us in our eternal progression? There are many answers to that question.[13] Let me mention two.

A. Making and keeping eternal covenants with God gives us the opportunity to complete our faith through action.

The *Lectures on Faith* make it clear that faith is "the principle of action."[14] Or, as Elder John A. Widtsoe put it: "Faith is a principle that demands action. . . . Otherwise it remains an idle belief, an abstract conviction, a theory."[15] Our faith is incomplete unless it is accompanied by action.[16] By entering into a promise to do something to demonstrate our faith and then by following up on that promise, we *complete* our faith, thereby making it a live, operative power in our lives.

Indeed, I believe that when we enter into gospel covenants, when we sincerely and honestly pledge to God to do something that He asks us to do, we instantly receive an increased ability to accomplish that task because we have exercised our faith in making that covenant. By agreeing to enter into a promise with the Lord, we manifest our faith in Him and our belief in His promises, and we thereby receive the power that always accompanies any exercise of faith in the Lord.[17]

It could not have been easy for the people of Ammon to decide to meet an armed force intent on their destruction by laying aside their weapons. Only great faith in God could have prompted such a decision. And surely that resolve must have been sorely tested as they watched, and in some cases directly experienced, the heavy sacrifice which their faith-inspired decision required. But just as surely, the fact that they had entered into a solemn covenant with God—and that they had in turn been promised by Him that if they kept His commandments they would in the long run be blessed eternally—increased their faith and gave them the strength to adhere to that faith-inspired covenant when the most trying moments arrived.

B. Entering into and keeping gospel covenants causes us to focus on the future when the haunting memories of the past or the immediate challenges of the present threaten to overwhelm us.

Covenants force us to look forward. That eternal, forward-looking perspective can give us strength to meet the trials we must all face in order to progress.

The decision of the people of Ammon to lay aside their swords was prompted in large part by the deep regret they felt for the "many sins" (Alma 24:10) that they had committed in the past. And these were not limited to minor mistakes. The list included the grievous sin of murder (see Alma 24:10–11). They were, by their own account, "the most lost of all mankind" (Alma 24:11). How easy it would have been for the people of Ammon to become mired in the debilitating but incorrect view that their sins were too serious to be overcome. How easy it is for us to be overwhelmed at times in our lives by the same satanic doctrine. In such moments, covenants give us hope just as they did to the people of Ammon by focusing us not on our past but on our glorious future—and, more important, on Him who makes that future possible. Covenants provide an immediate and ongoing reminder of our connection with the Savior, whose atoning sacrifice makes it possible for us to overcome all our past mistakes and gives us hope in all our futures.

Similarly, focusing on covenants can provide us with the eternal perspective we need when present difficulties seem unbearable. It was their firm belief that "if our brethren destroy us . . . , we shall go to our God and shall be saved" (Alma 24:16) that gave the people of Ammon the strength to faithfully meet the kind of challenge few of us will be required to face. Covenants shifted their focus from their immediate situation to the future happiness that was promised them if they kept their covenants. This in turn gave them the heavenly strength they needed to persevere.

Covenants thus enliven and strengthen our faith *and* give us the eternal perspective we need to overcome both our past and our present difficulties.

How Can We Increase Our Desire and Ability to Make and Keep Covenants?

Now to the final question: How can we increase our ability to keep our covenants so that the powers of heaven might be more available to us? Again, there are numerous answers, but let me focus on just one.

One of the best ways we can strengthen our ability to keep the covenants we have made is to reflect on those covenants often enough to make them an active, ongoing part of our lives. In that regard we would do well to take greater advantage of the wonderful opportunity we have each Sunday to partake of the sacrament. I believe that many of us underestimate both the importance of that sacred ordinance and the power—immediate daily power—that can come from greater focus on it.

I believe it is possible that the very frequency of the ordinance can cause us to overlook its significance.[18] We may too often view the opportunity to partake of the sacrament as merely a chance to renew our baptismal covenant, to wipe the slate clean, and to start over again. Now let me emphasize that that renewal is a great blessing in and of itself, but if we stop there, we may miss the full significance and the full power of that ordinance.

Elder Neil L. Andersen has recently taught: "Spirituality is not stagnant, and neither are covenants. Hopefully . . . all of us as members are moving along a progressive growth, both in our spirituality and in our covenants. Covenants bring not only commitments, but they bring spiritual power. . . . The sacrament is a beautiful time to not just renew our baptismal covenants but to commit to Him to renew all our covenants . . . and to approach Him in a spiritual power that we did not have previously."[19]

When we partake of the sacrament we can witness unto the Father (see D&C 20:77, 79; see also 3 Nephi 18:10–11)[20] that we remember all the covenants we have made and that we are willing to enter into them again, including the covenant that we will always remember His Son. And each week we receive His promise—as sure, as certain, as immutable a promise as has ever existed—that we will always have His Spirit to be with us to guide us, to strengthen us, and to change our very natures. Proper attention to the purpose and power of the sacrament can greatly increase the heavenly power that comes from keeping all of our covenants.

If we come to more fully understand and abide by our covenants, it will greatly change our lives. Moreover, the positive effects will not end with us; others will be directly impacted as well.

Some years after the people of Ammon made the remarkable decision to bury their weapons of war and to rely on their unique covenant with the Lord as a means of encountering a threat to their mortal existence, they found themselves in a similar situation when the Lamanites came to attack not just them but also the Nephites who were protecting them. Out of love for the Nephites they gave some thought to taking up arms to help defend their protectors (see Alma 53:13). But after being reminded of the importance of keeping that solemn covenant, they "were compelled to behold their brethren wade through their afflictions" (Alma 53:15; see also 14) without providing any direct military assistance—a sacrifice that must have been almost as difficult as what they had gone through years earlier.

However, recognizing that this particular covenant was unique to them, they realized that their own children—some of whom may not have been born at the time of the covenant and many of whom were now old enough to take up arms themselves—"had not entered into a covenant that they would not take their weapons of war to defend themselves" (Alma 53:16). And so these young men went to war. We are all familiar with their story. We call them the sons of Helaman because they were led by that great Nephite leader. But I think we would do well to also remember that they were really the sons of the people of Ammon. If we do not, we may overlook the profound and enduring impact that their parents' steadfast adherence to their unique covenant had on these young men.

In their first military tour of duty, these sons of the people of Ammon were in a situation in which they had to decide whether to fight or to flee. Helaman described their reaction and, more important, the source of their determination: "Now they never had fought, yet they did not fear death; and they did think more upon the liberty of their fathers than they did upon their lives; yea, they had been taught by their mothers, that if they did not doubt, God would deliver them. And they rehearsed unto me the words of their mothers, saying: We do not doubt our mothers knew it" (Alma 56:47–48).

Note that the scriptures do not indicate that these young men had no doubts of their own about God and His commandments. The faith of some of these young men may well have not been fully developed at that point in their lives, though it soon would be. But the one thing they did not doubt was that *their mothers knew it.* And what their mothers knew and taught so powerfully to them was "that if they did not doubt, *God would deliver them.*"

Think about that teaching in that context: "God would deliver them" if they *kept their covenant.* The Book of Mormon does not tell us much about the fathers of those whom we call the sons of Helaman. I suspect that one reason for that is that at least some of those sons grew up in homes without fathers, in families led by single mothers who had seen their husbands killed because of their steadfast commitment to their covenant with God.

And it was those sweet, valiant women whose words and

examples made it crystal clear to their sons that they knew "God would deliver" their sons if their sons would not doubt. Of all people, these mothers understood full well that the promise that God would deliver them did not mean that He would spare them from the immediate pains, afflictions, and disappointments of this life or even from the immediate effects of physical death itself. But they knew that in the most important, eternal sense—the only sense that really matters in the long run—God would surely deliver on His promise of exaltation if they simply did not doubt the power of that promise. And this truth was so deeply ingrained in the words, actions, and beings of those steadfast women that their sons *could not* doubt that their mothers knew it. And because their mothers knew, they too believed and acted on that belief.

This kingdom—the kingdom of God—will be built up by covenant-keeping, multigenerational families. That is what heaven will look like and that is what heaven on earth *can* look like. Gospel covenants open up the powers of heaven. And covenants open up those powers both for those who make and keep those covenants *and for those whom they love*. Of all the powers of heaven that are made available to those who keep sacred covenants, perhaps none is of greater importance than the eternal impact covenant keeping will have on their children, their grandchildren, and multiple generations to come.

I testify that God lives and that as surely as He lives He will fulfill His promises to us. If we will but believe in Him and manifest that belief by adhering to the covenants He offers us, the very powers of heaven will gather to aid us and our loved ones in whatever challenges we face.

Covenant Keepers and the Family of God

Camille Fronk Olson

When we talk about covenants, we're talking about family. When we talk about sisters and brothers as we meet together in the Church, we're talking about covenants that are made possible through the messenger of the covenant: Jesus Christ.

This past week I've learned a bit more about how real the connection is between family and covenant. My brother told me about a new program that they are trying in his ward where you can have your ward family history specialist log in as you and see what work has been done and what still needs to be done. So she logged in for my brother and dropped by their house to announce: "I can't believe it. You're right. It's all done." (No contribution from my part, I might add.)

At about the very same time that I learned that the saving ordinances for my ancestors have been completed several generations back, I received an e-mail from a man named Albert in Canada who was reaching out to see if we are related. He found me because of my unique last name, Fronk, which was spelled "Vruggink" before my ancestors emigrated from Holland. So

I became especially excited when I read that his mother was a Vruggink from the same city as my ancestors who left when they joined the Church. Albert also grew up in that same city in the Netherlands and remembers hearing his grandfather speak of a great-uncle who left their Dutch homeland in 1869 to come to Utah because of religion. When Albert immigrated to Canada in 1964, his uncle made him promise to discover what had happened to his grand-uncle's descendants who had come to Utah. I like to imagine my great-great-grandfather in the spirit world talking with his older brother about how we're going to get these kids of theirs talking to each other when they don't know about each other at all. And somehow this distant cousin, who is not a member of our faith, got the message and reached out. Suddenly my family tree has expanded. In truth I can never say, "We've gone as far as we can go in family history." There are people alive here on the earth right now who are part of that family. As a daughter of the covenant, I have promised to reach out and find ways to include and invite them to receive the same blessings. Of note, this distant relative reached out to me, not the other way around.

Another little exchange happened that has shaped my preparation for this conference. An acquaintance approached me to comment that she saw my name listed as speaking at Women's Conference. She told me that she noted from the program that I was said to be a mother. She took exception to it by saying, "Are you really a mother?" because she knew I had married later in life and did not bear a child. Actually, I inherited two children when I married their father, and all I can tell you is that Emily and Dave are family. I call those two "our children," not "mine." I don't know how I could love them more if I had given birth to them. Perhaps we worry too much about what eternal families look like in the hereafter and so we extrapolate too much about little details without understanding how God plans to work it out.

Anyway, these two experiences helped me see "family" more inclusively, broadly, and deeply in light of the Lord's covenant with us. Why do we try to be so literal when we ascribe family roles to others or to ourselves? We know that second marriages—after death or divorce, adoptions, whether formal or informal—exist in virtually every family now. Family trees are rarely a simple diagram of birth parents and children. So if someone tries to warn you against adoption or marriage because it will "mess up the family tree," tell them to get over it.

Covenants bind people together in ways beyond what blood can do. This is the plan of our Father in Heaven. He wants all of us to come into the fold and be together. It was definitely the case of our forefathers and foremothers in the ancient world that we read about in the Bible. Rather than following a direct bloodline in the era of the biblical patriarchs and matriarchs, faith in Jehovah and His covenants constituted "family."

Covenant meant everything to Adam and Eve. Succinctly and clearly, Samuel the Lamanite explained the reason why: "All mankind, by the fall of Adam being cut off from the presence of the Lord, are considered as dead, both as to things temporal and to things spiritual" (Helaman 14:16). Because of the Fall, humankind was considered dead to God. We like to sing "I Am a Child of God"[1] and with our Young Women stand and say, "We are daughters of a Heavenly Father who loves us,"[2] which both make reference to our premortal relationship to the Father of our spirits. By doing a little research in scripture, however, you will find that humankind is more often called children of men, or children of Adam, rather than children of God. Specifically, we are called "children of men" or a related descriptor more than 270 times in scripture, and called "children of God" only 62 times, 56 of which refer to our ability to *become* the children of God, rather than to our being spirit offspring of the Father.

Let me illustrate. When King Benjamin's people felt no more disposition to do evil, but to do good continually, they were ready to make a covenant with the Lord and thereby *become* His spiritually-adopted children. King Benjamin explained, "And now, because of the covenant which ye have made ye shall be called the children of Christ, his sons, and his daughters; for behold, this day he hath spiritually begotten you; for ye say that your *hearts* are *changed* through faith on his name" (Mosiah 5:7). That covenant was possible because of Jesus Christ and because of the people's hearts which changed through faith in Christ. Likewise, when we are baptized, we make a covenant to *become* part of God's family as adopted children of Christ.

Note what we find in the gospel according to John, "But as many as received him, to them gave he *power* to *become* the sons [and daughters] of God, even to them that believe on his name" (John 1:12; emphasis added). On condition of us receiving Him, the Redeemer grants us *power to become* his children. The Apostle Paul wrote that the Son of God was made of a woman "to redeem them that were under the law, that we might *receive* the *adoption* of sons [and daughters]" (Galatians 4:5). Paul testified that we could be "adopted" into God's family. He wrote something similar to the Romans, "For as *many* as are *led* by the Spirit of God, they are the sons [and daughters] of God" (Romans 8:14). Do you notice the condition again? Because of the condition, we know that this is not referring to our relationship with the Father in premortality. Paul continued, "Ye have received the Spirit of adoption, . . . and if children, then heirs; heirs of God, and joint-heirs with Christ" (Romans 8:15–17). Notice that Paul is teaching of a relationship that surpasses our being children of Christ; we can be adopted to become "children of God" (Romans 8:16). In the Doctrine and Covenants, Joseph Smith learned that through believing obedience we become *begotten* sons and daughters of God, or joint heirs with Christ (D&C 76:24). These and multiple additional passages of scripture allude to adoption into God's family through faith in Jesus Christ.

Because of the Fall, we are as if dead, cut off, and need to be born again, or spiritually begotten. President Joseph F. Smith taught this same doctrine this way: "The object of our earthly existence is that . . . we may become the sons and daughters of God, in the fullest sense of the word, being heirs of God and joint heirs with Jesus Christ, to be kings and priests unto God, to inherit glory, dominion, exaltation, thrones and every power and attribute developed and possessed by our Heavenly Father." We become like Him as a result. "This is the object of our being on this earth."[3]

Adam and Eve were the first to make that covenant and then teach it to their children. The covenant was then handed down from generation to generation and reestablished in Abraham's day. Abraham desired to have the blessings of the fathers not only for himself but to give to others, to invite others to receive those unparalleled blessings. His own father was not able to introduce these truths to him, so he had to seek them elsewhere. Who did he find to help him? Melchizedek.

As Jehovah made the covenant with Abraham, He explained what He promised to do for him and his family. "I will lead thee by my hand, and I will take thee, to put upon thee my name, even the Priesthood of thy father, and my power shall be over thee" (Abraham 1:18). From the Genesis account, we read, "I will establish my covenant between me and thee and thy seed after thee in their generations for an everlasting covenant, to be a God unto thee, and to thy seed after thee" (Genesis 17:7).

Abraham's wife, Sarah, was also included in the covenant (as were all who followed God's word), which Jehovah made very clear when He changed her name. Isaiah knew that truth when he wrote, "Ye that follow after righteousness, . . . look unto the rock whence ye are hewn. . . . Look unto Abraham your father, and unto Sarah that bare you" (Isaiah 51:1–2). Then Isaiah reiterated Jehovah's promise: "For the Lord shall comfort Zion: he will comfort all her waste places; and he will make her wilderness like Eden." Do you see the reversal that's promised with the covenant? Where there was desert, it becomes Eden. "Her desert like the garden of the Lord; joy and gladness shall be found therein, thanksgiving, and the voice of melody" (Isaiah 51:3). Or as Isaiah said it later, "Beauty for ashes" (Isaiah 61:3). So what is required of us? "Hearken unto me my people, and give ear unto me O my nation" (Isaiah 51:4). His people, His nation are therefore those who hearken, those who hear, and those who do what He commands (see D&C 29:7).

If you map out Abraham's lineage, you find that his is not

an easy, simple, uncluttered family tree. I want to review part of that family tree. Abraham receives the covenant. He's married to Sarah, who likewise makes the covenant, but Sarah is commanded by the Lord to also give Abraham another wife. So Abraham and Hagar have a son named Ishmael. When Ishmael is thirteen years old, the Lord makes the covenant with him. Remember that Ishmael was circumcised, which is the sign of the covenant, as were all the other men that belonged to Abraham's household (Genesis 17:23–27). When Hagar and Ishmael were later sent away, God did not forget them, part of what He promises in the covenant. He follows them and speaks to Hagar to give her a promise that Ishmael will be the father of a great nation from twelve sons (Genesis 21:17–21). I will return to Ishmael's descendants; they are part of the covenant.

Meanwhile, back to Sarah and Abraham. In their old age they had a son, Isaac. And Isaac married Rebekah, and Isaac and Rebekah gave birth to the twins Esau and Jacob. God spoke to Rebekah to inform her that the younger twin, Jacob, would lead the covenant in his generation, but Esau could also receive the covenant. Because Esau despised the covenant and the birthright, he married out of the covenant. After receiving his father's blessing to be the steward over the covenant, Jacob is sent away to go find himself a wife who will help him safeguard the covenant. He succeeds very well. Not just one, but why not four good wives? And they have twelve sons and at least one daughter.

Jacob's family forms the basis for what is called the nation of Israel. But that nation of Israel is not just those who are the direct lineage of these twelve tribes. Abraham later married a third wife, Keturah, who gave birth to six sons, one of whom was Midian (Genesis 25:1–4). One of Midian's descendants was Jethro, who ordained Moses with power and authority in the Holy Priesthood (D&C 84:6). Moses was a descendant from Levi, Leah's third son by Jacob, and Jethro has a daughter, Zipporah, and who does she marry? Moses (Exodus 2:16–22). So clearly we now have Midianites in the family of Israel.

There will soon be Canaanites in the family tree, including Rahab the harlot (Joshua 2; 6:25). She has a testimony of the Hebrew God, joins with the Israelites, and becomes an ancestress of Jesus Christ (Matthew 1:5). Moabites are also in the Israelite family tree through Ruth. There could have been other Moabites, too, as well as other peoples who joined with the people of Jehovah because they believed that He was the one true God.

But wait! There's more. Remember Esau? When he saw that his marrying out of the covenant disappointed his parents, he married a daughter of Ishmael (Genesis 28:6–9). If Ishmael and Hagar hadn't been blessed and enabled by God's covenant, the fact that Esau married one of his daughters would be insignificant. The descendants of the daughter of Ishmael and Esau are called the Edomites—or, in New Testament times, the Idumeans. Talk about a complicated and messy family tree!

Included in Abraham and Sarah's family tree, I see evidence that more than the stewards or generational leaders of this covenant received the blessings of the covenant. Consider Doctrine and Covenants 132: "Abraham received concubines, and they bore him children; and it was accounted unto him for righteousness" (can you see Hagar in there?) "because they were given unto him, and he abode in my law; as Isaac also and Jacob did none other things than that which they were commanded; and because they did none other things than that which they were commanded, they have entered into their exaltation, according to the promises, and sit upon thrones, and are not angels but are gods" (v. 37). Do Abraham, Isaac, and Jacob become gods alone? Marriage is an essential part of the "new and everlasting covenant" (D&C 131:1–4). In other words, according to these revelations, if Abraham, Isaac, and Jacob have been granted God's gift of exaltation, so have their wives.

Next, come with me to New Testament times where we find people who assume they have become children of God because they are direct descendants of Abraham. When some of the Jewish leaders said to Jesus, "Abraham is our father. Jesus saith unto them, If ye were Abraham's children, ye would do the works of Abraham" (John 8:39). In essence, Jesus told them that being numbered in God's family is not necessarily connected to blood relationships but rather to obedience. The Doctrine and Covenants relays a great definition of what it means to be "the elect" of God according to the covenant: The elect are those who "hear my voice and harden not their hearts" (D&C 29:7). Isn't that good? That's what covenant keepers do.

Now let's look at one or two New Testament examples of covenant keepers. My favorite example of such is Mary, the mother of Jesus. Certainly, she could talk about her blood relationship with Jesus and her royal lineage. She could pack the BYU Marriott Center time and time again as the expert on what it means to be the family of God. But I don't think she would be touting her family tree. When the angel first visited her to announce that she would be the mother of the Son of God, she referred to herself as "the handmaid of the Lord," and then promised, "be it unto me according to thy word" (Luke 1:38). She committed her will to the will of God. When she was carrying the Son of God and she met Elisabeth, and she discovered that Elisabeth knew through the spirit that Mary was also with child, Mary sang the wonderful *Magnificat*: "My soul doth magnify the Lord, and my spirit hath rejoiced in God my Saviour. . . . And his mercy is on them that fear him from generation to generation." She is singing of the covenant that endures from generation to generation. Mary continued, "He hath put down the mighty from their seats, and exalted them of low degree. He hath filled the hungry with good things; and the rich he hath sent empty away." Here we see signs of the covenant expressed as reversals again, like beauty for ashes. And then she sang, "He hath holpen . . ." The word translated by King James's scholars as *holpen* means more than "helped." It suggests taking by the hand, supporting, sustaining, and succoring. "He hath holpen his servant Israel, in remembrance of his mercy; as he spake to our fathers, to Abraham, and to his seed forever" (Luke 1:46–47, 50, 52–55). Yes, she sang of the promises of the covenant.

The gospels later imply that Mary's other sons did not support Jesus and His ministry and would therefore not honor the covenant (see Mark 3:21 ["friends" here is better translated "those of his household"]; John 7:5). Once when Jesus was in Galilee, his mother and his brothers came to see him. The crowd notified Jesus that his family was among the multitude. They appeared to have expected that Jesus would ask the crowd to give way, let them come up, because they had a special place as his family. But that isn't what happens. Instead, Jesus said,

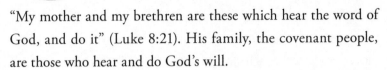

"My mother and my brethren are these which hear the word of God, and do it" (Luke 8:21). His family, the covenant people, are those who hear and do God's will.

Just a few chapters later, in the gospel of Luke, a woman of the company was likely thinking the same thing about Mary when she said to Jesus, "Blessed is the womb that bare thee, and the paps which thou hast sucked." In other words: blessed be your mother; she must be the most blessed of all. However, what does Jesus answer? "Yea rather, blessed are they that hear the word of God, and keep it" (Luke 11:27–28). He offered this woman the same explanation as He gave the multitude earlier. Obedience to God constitutes who are the children of God.

At the time of the crucifixion, when so many of the disciples scattered as sheep without a shepherd, confused and offended (see Matthew 26:31), we see Mary, the mother of Jesus, and a few other women standing by the cross of Jesus (see John 19:25). We don't hear her voice in this scene, but her stance speaks volumes. If you want an image of what it means to "stand for truth and righteousness," look at Mary on this occasion. She doesn't care what people will think of her because of the shame associated with crucifixion. Without flinching, she stoically exemplifies the meaning of hearkening to the voice of the Lord by standing as a disciple, a covenant keeper, for her Savior.

I wish we knew more of these great women and men in the Bible, but we receive only this little glimpse. After the forty-day ministry of the resurrected Christ, some 120 Saints came back to Jerusalem to meet with the apostles. Among those Saints were "women, and Mary the mother of Jesus, *and . . . his brethren* (Acts 1:14; emphasis added). Without knowing the background story of Mary's younger sons, we glimpse evidence of the blessings of the covenant. Something happened to those brothers during those forty days because they are there, numbered with the other believers, witnesses of the resurrection and divinity of Jesus Christ.

One quick look at a Book of Mormon example. You know about the faith that the stripling warriors learned from their mothers. But where did these mothers learn faith? They had made covenants with God when their hearts were changed to believe in Him. And once those mothers and fathers made covenants, they knew the truth and were firm, and they never turned away from it (see Alma 23:6; 24:11–19; 53:16–22; 56:46–48).

So here's my conclusion, my friends—may I say my family? I will summarize by listing four blessings that are manifest by covenant keepers in scripture that we may find in our own lives:

1. They recognize God's hand in their lives, day after day. Laman and Lemuel reacted to challenges in their day with sentiments such as, "Are you kidding? It's not fair. Why is this happening to me? Everyone else is back in Jerusalem having a wonderful time, and here I am with never-ending work to do. Why can't I be having fun back in Jerusalem?" Meanwhile, Nephi faced the same challenges with sentiments akin to, "Wow, check it out. We get to eat raw meat and it tastes sweet. When does that ever happen?" And if Nephi's saying that, I'll tell you who else is saying it even more: Sariah and the other women who no longer need to cook that meat. I can't help but think they were praising God for His hand in their lives.

2. They receive power to draw others to Christ and his covenant. Because there's a magnetism inherent in God's work, many

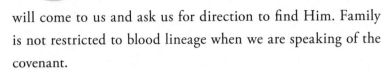

will come to us and ask us for direction to find Him. Family is not restricted to blood lineage when we are speaking of the covenant.

3. They develop an awareness and love for eternal family. Blessed by the perfect love of Christ, we can see family wherever we look. At this conference with me today are three nieces who returned from missions during the past year. Through Christlike service, they discovered eternal family in Finland, in Alabama, and in the Philippines.

4. We become children of God, his family, by making and keeping His covenants. We stand as witnesses for Him at all times, and in all things, and in all places. We find it a pleasure to serve Him and show compassion to those around us.

I pray that we may be true to what we have covenanted to do. May we pray for strength to harden not our hearts and hearken to his voice. May we remember Him who made it all possible. We are family. May we treat each other as such.

Women of Dedication, Faith, Determination, and Action

Elder M. Russell Ballard

William R. "Max" Carey Jr., founder of an *Inc.* 500 company, told this story: "Not long ago I had the chance to do something I've always wanted to do—meet my wife's boyfriend from high school. We'll call him Billy Bob. I had only seen photos of the guy. . . . Anyway, we're in my wife's hometown and we walk into the general store, and there is Billy Bob behind the counter. It turns out he's the store manager. After talking for a few minutes, I can hardly wait to get back into the car to hear Susan's reaction. I say, 'Gee, Susan, wasn't it great to see Billy Bob after all these years?' 'Uh-huh,' she replies. 'What did you think?' I ask. 'Nothing much,' she says. There is a long silence. I can't hold it in any longer. 'Susan,' I say, 'I've just got to ask you one question. Aren't you glad you married me? I mean, aren't you glad you're married to the CEO of a successful company instead of the manager of a general store?' Well, she looks at me as only a wife can and says, 'Let's get one thing straight here, Max. If I'd married Billy Bob, he'd be the CEO of a successful company, and *you* would be the manager of a general store.'"[1]

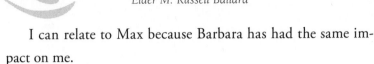

I can relate to Max because Barbara has had the same impact on me.

We laugh at this story because we know there is some truth in it—women really do have remarkable influence.

No one can do what you sisters can do to help move the gospel kingdom forward and make the world a better place. No one.

You have been divinely endowed with a unique kind of discernment and strength that differs in some ways from the gifts our Heavenly Father gave His sons. These differences are intentional and eternal. They don't make you better than a man, nor do they make you inferior to him. They just make you different—wonderfully, deliberately, everlastingly so.

When you join with other women of covenant in unity and harmony, there is no limit to your influence for good.

I have witnessed your significant and eternal influence in individual lives as well as in families, and I have seen it in countless cultures and countries around the globe. I have also seen what you can accomplish in branches, wards, stakes, missions, temples, and general Church assignments. Your contributions in small and large businesses and charities, as well as in civic, educational, health, and sports organizations, are immeasurable.

I am particularly impressed by your ability to nurture—to care for and encourage the healthy growth or development of others as you help shepherd them along the covenant path. This is a gift from God and is an important part of your divine endowment from a loving Heavenly Father.

Your efforts to nurture in the family, the Church, the school, the community, and in the professional world have been a blessing to many, including those who are deceived, lonely, hurt, sick, and aging. This is a Christlike attribute—a blessing to a world that desperately is in need of nurturing.

I have been the beneficiary of a lifetime of nurturing by the incredible women in my life, beginning with my mother and extending through the years to my wife, Barbara, my sisters, my daughters and daughters-in-law, my granddaughters, my friends and colleagues, and faithful women leaders with whom I am privileged to serve. For the next few minutes I would like to share with you some of what I have learned from these women of determination, faith, dedication, and action, in the hope that you may be as inspired by their insights as I have been.

It was twenty-two years ago that I spoke in conference both in April and October about the power of councils with faithful women participating. Your insight and counsel is absolutely essential. Today the Lord has richly blessed the Church and the world because there are more sister missionaries serving faithfully in mission leadership positions and participating in mission leadership councils. More are receiving their endowments earlier, thereby enlarging the number of temple covenant women serving in the Church. The sister leaders of the general presidencies pray and speak in general conference. And significantly, now the general women's meeting is the first session of general conference.

I know some women wish they could find more stories of women in the scriptures and in our history. We need to develop the skill to find their influence, like one young sister. She said, "Mormon must have had an amazing wife to have raised a remarkable son like Moroni!"

If you look carefully and with the right spirit, you can find

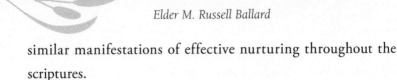

similar manifestations of effective nurturing throughout the scriptures.

For a number of years now, the Church has been focusing attention on the faithful sisters in the Church and their contributions. For example, I invite you to examine the topic of "Women of Conviction" on the Church History Library webpage.

Remember, the role of the pioneer sisters was remarkable. When writing about the Mormon pioneers, non-LDS author Wallace Stegner noted that he had admiration for the men, but stated, "Their women were incredible."[2]

As we look for and find women in our scriptures and in our history, we will see far better the power and influence women have in our family, community, the Church, and the world.

I realize that women often deal with a kind of ambiguity not necessarily faced by men, as there is an endless array of choices as well as uncertainties in front of you. This can be particularly challenging today because the world offers women an increasing number of opportunities— many more than were available to women a generation ago. In fact, in my lifetime we have seen numerous women appointed and elected to public offices, fill positions as CEOs of major corporations and organizations, and admitted in increasing numbers to prestigious business, law, and medical schools.

Joseph Smith said in 1842, "I now turn the key to you in the name of God, and this society shall rejoice and knowledge and intelligence shall flow down from this time—this is the beginning of better days [for women]."[3]

We are seeing the fulfillment of this prophetic vision as new opportunities and advancements for women unfold in unprecedented ways.

Women today are told that they can "have it all": education, careers, church service, marriage, and family. However, most women discover that this is not always true. As Meg Whitman, an American business executive and political candidate, once said in reference to the question of whether you can have it all, "I actually don't think so. I think you can have a wonderful life, but you have to decide what trade-offs you're willing to make."[4]

Balancing everything among all of the available options can be a challenge. In the end, most of us have to choose among competing options to determine what is best for us.

Of course, we have a divine pattern to follow as outlined in "The Family: A Proclamation to the World," but we know that mortality can be complicated. Many women are single for long periods of time in their lives. Some women are married; others become single when a spouse dies or when they divorce. And some women may never marry.

Nevertheless, if we are faithful and endure to the end, no righteous desire will be denied, and all blessings—allow me to repeat that for emphasis—*all blessings* ultimately will be received.

Each of you must come to know what the Lord wants for you individually, given the choices before you. Sister Julie B. Beck said, "The ability to qualify for, receive, and act on personal revelation is the single most important skill that can be acquired in this life."[5] I agree with her.

Once you know the Lord's will, you can then move forward in faith to fulfill your individual purpose. One sister may be inspired to continue her education and attend medical school,

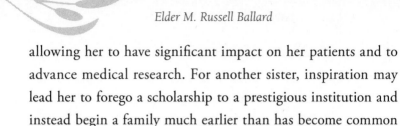

allowing her to have significant impact on her patients and to advance medical research. For another sister, inspiration may lead her to forego a scholarship to a prestigious institution and instead begin a family much earlier than has become common in this generation, allowing her to make a significant and eternal impact on her children now.

Is it possible for two similarly faithful women to receive such different responses to the same basic questions? Absolutely! What's right for one woman may not be right for another. That's why it is so important that we should not question each other's choices or the inspiration behind them. And we should refrain from asking hurtful and unsupportive questions like "Why are you going on a mission?" or "Why aren't you on a mission?" or "Why aren't you married?" or "Why don't you have children?" We can all be kinder and more thoughtful of the situations in which our sisters throughout the world find themselves as they seek to follow the will of our Heavenly Father in their individual lives.

Of course, it isn't always easy to refrain from questioning. That is especially true when our sisters and brothers make choices that seem to us to be wrong. For example, during the April general conference this year, a handful of men and women voiced their opposition to the sustaining of the First Presidency and the Quorum of the Twelve Apostles. While it was inappropriate in that setting to actually vocalize their opposition, it was certainly within their respective rights to oppose. If that were not so, why would we ask for a dissenting response each and every time we sustain Church leaders?

As members of the Church, we should not be critical of

those who have sincere, heartfelt questions or concerns about their faith. Remember, the Restoration in all of its glory and wonder was launched in response to a spiritual question of a fourteen-year-old young man. Such questions can be a catalyst to real conversion if they prompt us to seek truth in the light of faith.

In that respect, the Prophet Joseph Smith provides a good example of how to find answers when we have concerns, questions, and even doubts. He wanted to know if he could receive forgiveness, and he wanted to know which church was true so he could join it. In a very real sense, the Restoration was launched by young Joseph, who felt unsure of the doctrine he was learning in the Christian churches of his day and was unsatisfied by the answers and explanations he was getting.

He later explained, "The teachers of religion of the different sects understood the same passages of scripture so differently as to destroy all confidence in settling the question by an appeal to the Bible" (Joseph Smith–History 1:12).

He added, "At length I came to the conclusion that I must either remain in darkness and confusion, or else I must do as James directs, that is, ask of God" (JS–H 1:13).

And that, ultimately, is where Joseph Smith found the answer to the questions of his soul. He found inspiration through reading the words of the holy scriptures. But he found the truth on his knees in a grove of trees near his home.

Today we live in a world in which people don't ask of God— they seem to want to ask of Google. Even when it comes to questions of faith, there are many who trust the Internet to provide accurate, fair, and balanced answers to their questions more than

they trust the ultimate source of truth, our Heavenly Father. It's as if they believe that the scripture in James actually says, "If any of you lack wisdom, let him ask of the Internet."

Please don't misunderstand, sisters. I am not saying that we should never search the Internet for information about the Church's history, its teachings and doctrine. What I am saying is that we need to be prudent and careful about seeking answers to spiritually important questions online. We've all heard people make jokes and sarcastic comments about how you can't trust everything you read on the Internet. There's a good reason for that. It's no wonder that many people emerge from their online search for religious truth feeling surrounded by the same kind of "darkness and confusion" that Joseph Smith felt after talking to the various religious teachers of his time.

In his book *The Cult of the Amateur: How Today's Internet Is Killing Our Culture*, Andrew Keen compares the *Encyclopedia Britannica*, a professionally researched and edited work by experts who rely upon the best scholarship of our day, with certain popular Internet sources that do not distinguish between expert and untrained contributors and often blur the distinction between careful scholarship and biased opinions.[6]

Doesn't it make sense, sisters, to carefully consider the source of the information, especially in regard to matters of eternal significance? None of us here today would solicit medical advice for a family member with a life-threatening illness from an untrained or unlicensed person posing as a medical expert. We seek information from those who are trained with appropriate medical and health service degrees from accredited institutions. Even then, we would likely seek a second opinion.

Why then would we trust our faith and our eternal souls to websites that contain information posted by ill-informed or biased bloggers posing as experts, and predatory propagandists who seek to destroy faith—faith in God, faith in Jesus Christ, faith in the Bible, and faith in the restored Church of Jesus Christ?

Paul warned the early Saints not to be "tossed to and fro, and carried about with every wind of doctrine, by the sleight of men, and cunning craftiness, whereby they lie in wait to deceive" (Ephesians 4:14). Today the Internet is full of those lying in wait to deceive the uninformed and inexperienced.

In our search for gospel truth, we not only need to find reliable sources but we also need to give the Lord equal time in our daily pursuits. We need to study the scriptures and the words of the Lord's servants. We need to be living right before God—we need to be doing His will (see John 7:16–17). And we can never overstate the importance of taking our spiritual concerns directly to God and trusting His inspiration and guidance.

But then, most of you already knew that, didn't you? You are here at this women's conference not because you doubt, but because you believe—or because you want to believe. I commend you for your desire to fortify your faith with the information and testimonies that have been shared with you here, and I salute you for the powerful goodness of your lives. I celebrate your spirit, your intelligence, your compassion, and your integrity. I love that you can be unified in faith and purpose without sacrificing your individuality or your diversity. We need you, all of you, individually and collectively, for the service that you as a unique, individual daughter of God can render, drawing upon

your distinctive strengths and talents, insights and experiences, priorities and perspectives.

Remember the Apostle Paul's teaching on this subject when he said that the body of Christ (meaning the Church) is composed of many members. He said, "[Shall the foot] say, Because I am not the hand, I am not of the body . . . ? If the whole body were an eye, where [was] the hearing? . . . And the eye cannot say unto the hand, I have no need of thee" (see 1 Corinthians 12:15, 17, 21).

He explained the difference in this way: "God set the members every one of them in the body, as it hath pleased Him" (1 Corinthians 12:18).

Given the differences among the various members in the body, Paul pled with the Saints that "there should be no schism . . . the members should have the same care one for another" (1 Corinthians 12:25).

I invite you devoted sisters today to make sure that no schism or division exists within your families or your Church congregations, even with regards to such potentially divisive subjects as the current conversation regarding women and the priesthood. Church leaders have clarified this doctrine, so let us deal patiently with one another and treat each other with Christian kindness and respect despite our strong feelings and deep differences that may exist. Our focus should seek a perspective that embraces all of eternity, not just the here and now.

President Harold B. Lee once said the Church is the scaffold with which we build eternal families.[7] Elder L. Tom Perry observed, "There are two principal reasons why I appreciate President Lee's metaphor for the Church—as scaffolding for our eternal families. First, it helps me understand what the Church is. Second, and equally important, I understand what the Church is not."[8]

That's an interesting perspective, isn't it? Although the Church plays a pivotal role in proclaiming, announcing, and administering the necessary ordinances of salvation and exaltation, all of that, as important as it is, is really just the scaffolding being used in an infinite and eternal construction project to build, support, and strengthen the family. And just as scaffolding is eventually taken down and put away to reveal the final completed building, so too will the mortal, administrative functions of the Church eventually fade as the eternal family comes fully into view. In that context, it's important to remember that our Church assignments are only temporary, and that at some point we will all be released either by our leaders or by death. But we will never be released from our eternal callings within the family.

If members of the Church who worship in the temple are attuned, they will come to realize that the Lord has marvelous blessings in store for His faithful daughters and sons throughout eternity.

And what are those blessings? This contextual insight from Elder Dallin H. Oaks explains, "The purpose of mortal life and the mission of The Church of Jesus Christ of Latter-day Saints is to prepare the sons and daughters of God for their destiny—to become like our heavenly parents."[9]

He adds, "The purpose of The Church of Jesus Christ of Latter-day Saints is to help all of the children of God understand their potential and achieve their highest destiny. This church

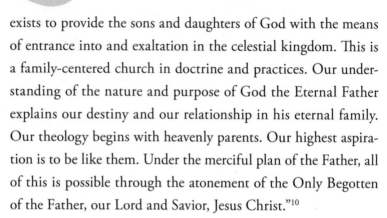

exists to provide the sons and daughters of God with the means of entrance into and exaltation in the celestial kingdom. This is a family-centered church in doctrine and practices. Our understanding of the nature and purpose of God the Eternal Father explains our destiny and our relationship in his eternal family. Our theology begins with heavenly parents. Our highest aspiration is to be like them. Under the merciful plan of the Father, all of this is possible through the atonement of the Only Begotten of the Father, our Lord and Savior, Jesus Christ."[10]

This is extraordinary doctrine, my dear sisters, both in its supernal majesty as well as its fundamental simplicity. The gospel story is a family story—nothing really more, or nothing less. It begins with heavenly parents, and it ends with children making their way through the sometimes exhilarating, sometimes overwhelming challenges of mortality and back to their heavenly home, having received all of the essential ordinances of eternal exaltation.

That's the story of our lives. God has given us the outline, but He leaves it up to us to flesh out the details through our choices and our faithfulness. There is an extraordinarily happy ending in store for all who desire it. But before we can claim it, we have to become more than just His children—we have to become His disciples.

Of course it is a remarkable thing to know that all of you sisters are daughters of our Heavenly Father, who loves you, and you love Him. But let's face it: you didn't have to do anything to become His daughter. You just *are*, and you always shall be. But you *do* have to do something to become His disciple. You have to choose to believe. You have to choose to follow the prophets and apostles. You have to choose to bend your will to His. You have to choose to have faith now and forever.

Being His daughter is a matter of birth. Being His disciple is a matter of choice, and the righteous exercise of your God-given agency.

That said, let me pose an all-important question: What matters most in our discipleship?

Life is filled with distractions that have potential to lead us away from the core teachings of the Church—especially the Atonement of Jesus Christ. I have observed that many of those who start to lose the Spirit have forgotten the very reasons they embraced the gospel in the first place. For the vast majority of us, the prime reason we accept baptism and the other ordinances and participate in this work with all our hearts, minds, and strength, has little to do with policy or programs. We did not join the Church because of its position on social issues or because of past practices. We joined the Church because of the gospel's core and eternal message. We joined the Church because the Spirit bore witness that the Prophet Joseph really did kneel in a grove of trees and did see the Father and the Son, and that the Savior's Church in its fulness has been restored.

The Prophet Joseph Smith said this: "The fundamental principles of our religion are the testimony of the Apostles and Prophets, concerning Jesus Christ, that He died, was buried, and rose again the third day, and ascended into heaven; and all other things which pertain to our religion are only appendages to it."[11]

The Atonement of Jesus Christ is at the heart of our message! It is our core value. It is our doctrinal center. It is the heart and soul of The Church of Jesus Christ of Latter-day Saints.

During the last U.S. presidential campaign, media attention around the world focused on the Church in unprecedented ways. One of our mission presidents and his wife discovered that during their visits to universities, churches, and civic groups, and during their interviews for TV, radio, and newspapers, people wanted to focus on things that obscured our message.

They found it helpful to publicly read the sacramental prayers and remind those listening that these are the most quoted prayers and the most quoted scriptures in the Church, and that the administration of the sacramental emblems is the most repeated ordinance in the Church from Alaska to Argentina and from Australia to Asia.

In this ordinance, Latter-day Saints promise to always remember the Atonement of Jesus Christ. They take upon themselves the Savior's name and promise to keep His commandments and always remember Him.

If any one of you has not yet felt the truth and the power of the Savior's Atonement in your life, I invite you to refocus on the central message of the Restoration—a message declaring that we can be "made perfect through Jesus the mediator of the new covenant, who wrought out this perfect atonement through the shedding of his own blood" (D&C 76:69).

Sisters, please do whatever is necessary to stay focused on the simple and central message of the Restoration. Accept it. Understand it. Embrace it. Love it. Share it. Defend it.

After the Atonement, there are a number of other spiritually important things that can help us remain strong and faithful and focused in our discipleship. These things include personal and sincere daily prayer and thoughtful scripture reading, regular fasting with a purpose, and worshipping at church and in the temple.

The First Presidency and the Twelve Apostles want proper preparation and thoughtful partaking of the sacrament on a regular basis to help keep our members anchored to the Lord Jesus Christ and His gospel.

I am not talking about merely attending sacrament meeting. I am talking about worshipping Heavenly Father and the Savior in sacrament meeting. We worship Them in sacrament meeting by singing, praying, meditating, listening carefully to the sacramental prayers, and partaking of the sacrament, which prepares us spiritually for the coming week. We must prepare ourselves and our families a long time before the meeting begins, to have a spiritual experience that binds our hearts to our Lord and Savior Jesus Christ.

Sisters, this is just one hour in the week to reflect upon your lives. You might think of it as having a personal interview with yourselves with no smart phones, no tablets, no distractions!

As noted earlier, we partake of the sacrament repeatedly, as often as forty-eight times each year. Added up, a lifetime of partaking of the emblems of the Atonement of the Lord Jesus Christ can bring us precious blessings.

Last October in general conference, I pleaded with all the members of the Church to "stay in the boat and hold on!"[12] I promise you in the name of the Lord and through the apostolic keys I bear that no safer place can be found in all the world than in keeping the covenants you have made to follow the Father and His Son and those who hold the keys of the priesthood. If

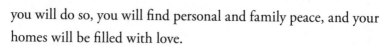

you will do so, you will find personal and family peace, and your homes will be filled with love.

Now my sisters, in closing you knew I would ask you to do something. I'm just asking you to do the same thing that the Prophet Joseph Smith asked the Relief Society sisters to do in Nauvoo when he said, "The [Relief] Society is not only to relieve the poor, but to save souls."[13]

"Every sister in this Church who has made covenants with the Lord has a divine mandate to help save souls, to lead the women of the world, to strengthen the homes of Zion, and to build the kingdom of God."[14] Please help us to keep the Church moving forward with increased faith in the lives of our individual members.

Righteous and faithful women have always played an essential role in saving souls and defending the kingdom of God. However, you women of this last dispensation have especially important roles and responsibilities to fulfill. You are women of determination, faith, dedication, and action.

Listen to the testimony of Jane Robinson, a nineteenth-century English convert: "I believed in the principle of the gathering [to Zion] and felt it my duty to go although it was a severe trial to me, in my feeling to leave my native land and the pleasing associations that I had formed there; but my heart was fixed. I knew in whom I had trusted and with the fire of Israel's God burning in my bosom, I forsook home."[15]

Today, all of you sisters have spiritual roots that go back to Kirtland and Nauvoo. Even though you may not trace your personal family history back to those amazing sister-disciples, you are spiritually heirs to the same blessings because you have received the same ordinances and have made the same covenants.

You have been baptized into the Lord's Church. You have received the gift of the Holy Ghost, and many of you have been endowed and some of you have been sealed in the house of the Lord.

Like faithful sisters in the past, you need to learn how to use the priesthood authority with which you have been endowed to obtain every eternal blessing that will be yours.

Today more than ever, we need faithful, dedicated sister-Saints who, like Jane Robinson, have hearts that are fixed, who trust in the Lord, and who "with the fire of Israel's God burning in [their bosoms]" are willing to save souls and build the kingdom of God.

On behalf of the First Presidency and the Quorum of the Twelve, I extend our love to each and every one of you. I ask our Heavenly Father to bless you that you may have the peace and the calm assurance that what you do within The Church of Jesus Christ of Latter-day Saints is essential to the growth and the preparation of this world for that day when the Lord and Savior whom we all love will say, "It is enough," and will come to rule and reign. May every righteous desire of your hearts be granted unto you as I leave you my witness and my testimony that this Church is the Church of Jesus Christ, Joseph is His prophet of the Restoration, and Thomas S. Monson is His prophet today. The work will roll forward, but it cannot fulfill its true destiny without rolling forward hand in hand with you faithful, wonderful sisters of the Church, to which I witness and testify.

Notes

Delighting in Our Covenants
Wendy Watson Nelson

1. President David O. McKay said: "I believe there are few, even temple workers, who comprehend the full meaning and power of the temple endowment. Seen for what it is, it is the step-by-step ascent into the Eternal Presence" (quoted in Truman G. Madsen, *The Highest in Us* [Salt Lake City: Deseret Book, 1978], 103).

    President Marion G. Romney said: "When Jacob traveled from Beersheba toward Haran, he had a dream in which he saw himself on the earth at the foot of a ladder that reached to heaven where the Lord stood above it. He beheld angels ascending and descending thereon, and Jacob realized that the covenants he made with the Lord there were the rungs on the ladder that he himself would have to climb in order to obtain the promised blessings—blessings that would entitle him to enter heaven and associate with the Lord.

    "Because he had met the Lord and entered into covenants with him there, Jacob considered the site so sacred that he named the place Bethel, a contraction of Beth-Elohim, which means literally 'the House of the Lord,'" ("Temples—The Gates to Heaven," *Ensign*, March 1971, 16).

2. "There is no gift greater than the gift of salvation" (D&C 6:13).

NOTES

3. "My soul delighteth in the covenants of the Lord" (2 Nephi 11:5).

4. D. Todd Christofferson, "The Power of Covenants," *Ensign*, May 2009, 22.

5. Joseph Smith, *History of The Church of Jesus Christ of Latter-day Saints,* 7 vols., edited by B. H. Roberts (Salt Lake City: The Church of Jesus Christ of Latter-day Saints, 1932–51), 4:604.

6. Jeffrey R. Holland, "Place No More for the Enemy of My Soul," *Ensign*, May 2010, 45.

7. Holland, "The Ministry of Angels," *Ensign*, November 2008, 30.

8. See Neal A. Maxwell, "Premortality, a Glorious Reality," *Ensign*, November 1985, 15–18; Maxwell, "Meeting the Challenges of Today," Brigham Young University devotional, 10 October 1978, speeches. byu.edu; David B. Haight, "Temples and the Work Therein," *Ensign*, November 1993, 59; Dallin H. Oaks, "The Great Plan of Happiness," *Ensign*, November 1993, 72.

9. See Maxwell, "Premortality, a Glorious Reality," 15–18.

10. Truman G. Madsen, personal communication, 1995.

11. See John A. Widtsoe, "The Worth of Souls," Utah Genealogical and Historical Magazine, October 1934, 189.

12. See Carlfred Broderick, *The Uses of Adversity* (Salt Lake City: Deseret Book, 2008), 9.

13. Elder David B. Haight taught: "Saints of all ages have had temples in one form or another. There is evidence that temple worship was customary from Adam to Noah and that after the Flood the holy priesthood was continued; therefore, we have every reason to believe the ordinances of the temple were available to those entitled to receive them" ("Personal Temple Worship," *Ensign*, May 1993, 24; see also John A. Widtsoe, "Temple Worship," *Utah Genealogical and Historical Quarterly*, April 1921, 52).

14. Said Elder David B. Haight: "The gospel in its fulness was revealed to Adam. . . . [And] faithful members who understand the eternal nature of the gospel—of God's holy purpose to bring to pass the eternal life of man—understand clearly why the history of man seems to revolve around the building and use of temples" ("Personal Temple Worship," 23–24; see also Widtsoe, "Temple Worship," 53–54).

15. See Dale G. Renlund, "Latter-day Saints Keep on Trying," *Ensign*, May 2015, 56–58.

16. See Richard G. Scott, "The Joy of Redeeming the Dead," *Ensign*, November 2012, 93–95.

17. Ibid., 95.

18. Ibid.

19. God is indeed a great compensator. I achieved my highest score in Scrabble after setting it aside for two months and spending my previous "Scrabble time" in family history research.

20. Gordon B. Hinckley, "'An Humble and a Contrite Heart,'" *Ensign*, November 2000, 89.

21. Boyd K. Packer, *Mine Errand from the Lord* (Salt Lake City: Deseret Book, 2008), 196.

22. In Melvin J. Ballard, *Melvin J. Ballard: Crusader for Righteousness* (Salt Lake City: Bookcraft, 1966), 133.

23. Hinckley, "'An Humble and a Contrite Heart,'" 89.

24. Russell M. Nelson, "Covenants," *Ensign*, November 2011, 88.

25. Linda K. Burton, "The Power, Joy, and Love of Covenant Keeping," *Ensign*, November 2013, 113; Carole M. Stevens, "We Have Great Reason to Rejoice," *Ensign*, November 2013, 117.

26. "Those who struggle with [sin of any kind] may be disappointed in themselves, but the Savior is not disappointed with any who earnestly seek to repent" (Nelson, "To Change Minds and Hearts," Training Seminar for Mission Presidents, 17 February 2015).

27. See Robert J. Matthews, "Our Covenants with the Lord," *Ensign*, December 1980, 33–39.

28. President Boyd K. Packer said: "No member of this Church—and that means each one of you—will ever make a serious mistake without first being warned by the promptings of the Holy Ghost" ("How to Survive in Enemy Territory," *New Era*, April 2012, 3).

29. "Timid souls must learn to be brave; overzealous natures must develop patience; rebellious persons must learn to conform; the slothful must become diligent; the spiritually uncultured must be refined; and all must learn self-discipline" (Matthews, "Our Covenants with

the Lord," 35; see also Tad R. Callister, *Infinite Atonement* [Salt Lake City: Deseret Book, 2000], 220–49).

30. Holland, "The Laborers in the Vineyard," *Ensign*, May 2012, 33.

31. See "Safeguards for Using Technology" and "Missionary Work in the Digital Age," njmm.org.

An Exchange of Love between God and Us
Bonnie L. Oscarson

1. D. Todd Christofferson, "The Power of Covenants," *Ensign*, May 2009, 20.

2. Ibid.

3. Neal A. Maxwell, "Encircled in the Arms of His Love," *Ensign*, November 2002, 16.

4. Jeffrey R. Holland, "'This Do In Remembrance of Me,'" *Ensign*, November 1995, 67–68; paragraphing altered; quoting Joseph Fielding Smith, *Doctrines of Salvation*, comp. Bruce R. McConkie, 3 vols., (Salt Lake City: Bookcraft, 1954–56), 2:340.

5. Carlos E. Asay, "Temple Blessings and Applications," BYU Religious Education Faculty Meeting, March 6, 1998.

6. Boyd K. Packer, *The Holy Temple* (Salt Lake City: Bookcraft, 1980), 75.

7. Asay, "The Temple Garment: 'An Outward Expression of an Inward Commitment,'" *Ensign*, August 1997, 22.

8. Personal correspondence to author, 2011.

9. Donald L. Staheli, "Obedience—Life's Greatest Challenge," *Ensign*, May 1998, 82.

10. Donald L. Hallstrom, "The Heart and a Willing Mind," Brigham Young University devotional, 7 December 2010; available at https://speeches.byu.edu/talks/donald-l-hallstrom_the-heart-and-a-willing-mind/.

11. Ibid.

12. *Preparing to Enter the Holy Temple* (Salt Lake City: The Church of Jesus Christ of Latter-day Saints, 2002), 35.

13. Personal correspondence to author, 2011.

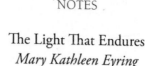

The Light That Endures
Mary Kathleen Eyring

1. Janice Kapp Perry, "I'm Trying to Be like Jesus," *Children's Songbook* (Salt Lake City: The Church of Jesus Christ of Latter-day Saints, 1989), 78.
2. O. Henry, "The Gift of the Magi," in *The Four Million* (New York: Doubleday, Page & Company, 1915), 25.
3. Jeffrey R. Holland, "Because of Your Faith," *Ensign*, November 2010, 7.

The Safety, Comfort, and Peace of Jesus
Laurel Christensen Day

1. Jeffrey R. Holland, "The Atonement of Jesus Christ," *Ensign,* March 2008, 34.
2. Holland, "Where Justice, Love, and Mercy Meet," *Ensign,* May 2015, 105.

"Help Thou Mine Unbelief"
Fiona Givens

1. Eugene Campbell and Richard D. Poll, *Hugh B. Brown: His Life and Thought* (Salt Lake City: Bookcraft, 1975), 196.
2. *Lectures on Faith* (Salt Lake City: Deseret Book, 1985), 38.
3. Tom Hooper, director, *Les Misérables* (Los Angeles: Universal, 2012).
4. Julian of Norwich, *The Showings of Julian of Norwich*, Denise N. Baker, ed. (W. W. Norton, 2005), 67.
5. See, for example, W. G. Wilson and J. H. Templeton, "Anglican Teaching: An Exposition of The Thirty-Nine Articles"; available at http://newscriptorium.com/assets/docs/anglican/39-articles /wtangteaching.htm.
6. Sigmund Freud, *Civilization and its Discontents,* (New York: W. W. Norton, 1989), 33.
7. Dietrich Bonhoeffer to Eberhard Berthge, 16 July 1944. In Larry L. Rasmussen, *Dietrich Bonhoeffer: Reality and Resistance* (Louisville, KY: Westminster John Knox Press, 2005), 83.

Repentance: A Fresh View
Kathryn Louise Callister

1. Bible Dictionary, s.v. "Repentance," 760.
2. Joseph Fielding Smith, *The Restoration of All Things* (Salt Lake City: Deseret Book, 1945), 196–97.
3. Gordon B. Hinckley, "Speaking Today: Excerpts from Recent Addresses of President Gordon B. Hinckley," *Ensign*, August 1996, 60.
4. Nita Dale Milner, "When I Am Baptized," *Children's Songbook* (Salt Lake City: The Church of Jesus Christ of Latter-day Saints, 1989), 103.
5. Richard G. Scott, "Finding Forgiveness," *Ensign*, May 1995, 75.
6. Scott, "Finding the Way Back," *Ensign*, May 1990, 74.
7. Tad R. Callister, *The Infinite Atonement* (Salt Lake City: Deseret Book, 2000), 189.
8. Vaughn J. Featherstone, "'Forgive Them, I Pray Thee,'" *Ensign*, October 1980, 30; emphasis added.
9. Robert L. Eaton and Henry Eyring, *I Will Lead You Along: The Life of Henry B. Eyring* (Salt Lake City: Deseret Book, 2013), 150.
10. Boyd K. Packer, "The Brilliant Morning of Forgiveness," *Ensign*, November 1995, 19.
11. Truman Madsen, *Christ and the Inner Life* (Salt Lake City: Bookcraft, 1978), 14; emphasis added.
12. Thomas S. Monson, "To the Rescue," *Ensign*, May 2001, 49.
13. Jeffrey R. Holland, "'Remember Lot's Wife': Faith Is for the Future," Brigham Young University devotional address, 13 January 2009; available at https://speeches.byu.edu/talks/jeffrey-r-holland _remember-lots-wife/.
14. Neil L. Andersen, "'Repent . . . That I May Heal You,'" *Ensign*, November 2009, 42.
15. See Al Fox Carraway, https://www.facebook.com/SpreadTheSpirit /photos/a.417241821706883.1073741825.347626828668383 /419712964793102/.
16. Andersen, "'Repent . . . That I May Heal You,'" 41.

Repentance: The Pathway to Perfection
Tad R. Callister

1. See http://www.oxforddictionaries.com/us/definition/american_english/peruse.

2. Dallin H. Oaks, *The Lord's Way* (Salt Lake City: Deseret Book, 1991), 223.

3. David O. McKay, cited in A. Theodore Tuttle, "Repentance," *Improvement Era*, November 1968, 64.

4. Ezra Taft Benson, "Preparing Yourselves for Missionary Service," *Ensign*, May 1985, 36.

5. Lest there be any misunderstanding, this does not eliminate the need for confession when required, because confession is often necessary to both hasten and complete the repentance process.

6. Charles Dickens, *A Christmas Carol* (London: Bradbury & Evans, 1858), 90.

7. See Boyd K. Packer, *The Things of the Soul* (Salt Lake City: Deseret Book, 1996), 116.

8. George Q. Cannon, *Gospel Truth: Discourses and Writings of President George Q. Cannon*, Jerreld L. Newquist, comp. (Salt Lake City: Deseret Book, 1957), 155.

9. Ibid.; emphasis added.

The Small but Important Things
Peggy S. Worthen

1. *Merriam-Webster Online Dictionary*, s.v. "wind sprint," merriam-webster.com/dictionary/wind%20sprint.

2. Ibid., s.v. "beta-endorphin," merriam-webster.com/dictionary/beta-endorphin.

3. Richard G. Scott, "Make the Exercise of Faith Your First Priority," *Ensign,* November 2014, 92–93.

Covenants Connect Us to Heaven
Kevin J Worthen

1. Walter F. González, "Followers of Christ," *Ensign*, May 2011, 14; citing Joseph Smith, *Joseph Smith* [manual], in Teachings of Presidents of the Church series (Salt Lake City: The Church of Jesus Christ of Latter-day Saints, 2007), 42n15. President Spencer W. Kimball observed: "We made vows, solemn vows, in the heavens before we came to this mortal life. . . . We have made covenants. We made them before we accepted our position here on earth" ("Be Ye Therefore Perfect," devotional address, Salt Lake Institute of Religion, University of Utah, 10 January 1975).

2. Online *Black's Law Dictionary,* s.v. "covenant," thelawdictionary.org /covenant.

3. Bible Dictionary, s.v. "Covenant," 651.

4. In some limited situations, the law does require the breaching party to honor the promise made rather than merely paying damages. See online *Black's Law Dictionary,* s.v. "specific performance," thelaw dictionary.org/specific-performance.

5. *Handbook 2: Administering the Church* (Salt Lake City: The Church of Jesus Christ of Latter-day Saints, 2010), 2.1.3, "Covenants"; emphasis added.

6. See Bruce C. Hafen, "Covenant Marriage," *Ensign,* November 1996, 26.

7. Ibid.

8. Ibid., quoting John 10:12–13.

9. See also JST, Genesis 14:30: God swore "unto Enoch and unto his seed with an oath by himself."

10. As the final verse of the hymn "How Firm a Foundation" makes clear, "The soul that on Jesus hath leaned for repose" has God's promise that He "will not, [He] cannot, desert to his foes." He promises "that soul, though all hell should endeavor to shake," that He will "never, no never, no never forsake!" (*Hymns of The Church of Jesus Christ of Latter-day Saints* [Salt Lake City: The Church of Jesus Christ of Latter-day Saints, 1985], no. 85).

11. "God having sworn unto Enoch . . . with an oath by himself; that every one being ordained after this order and calling should have power, by faith" (JST, Genesis 14:30).

12. See Hafen, "Covenant Marriage," 26.

13. See D. Todd Christofferson, "The Power of Covenants," *Ensign,* May 2009, 19–23.

14. *Lectures on Faith* (Salt Lake City: Deseret Book, 1985), 1.

15. John A. Widtsoe, "What Is the Need of Ordinances," in *Evidences and Reconciliation: Aids to Faith in a Modern Day* (Salt Lake City: Bookcraft, 1943), 197.

16. "Faith without works" truly "is dead," as James observed (James 2:20; see also James 2:17).

17. As an illustration, in Mosiah 18 we find the familiar verses that describe the terms of the baptismal covenant—the things we promise to do when we enter into that covenant with God. Note, however, that even before they entered into the baptismal covenant, the people of Alma were already "desirous to come into the fold of God" (v. 8). They were already "willing to bear one another's burdens, . . . to mourn with those that mourn," and to "comfort those that [stood] in need of comfort" (vv. 8–9). Alma asked them to enter into the baptismal covenant because this was already "the desire of [their] hearts" (v. 10). What they were doing was putting into action the faith that they had already developed in their hearts. And in return for their willingness to act on that faith by entering into that covenant through baptism, God promised that He would help them act on this desire by "pour[ing] out his Spirit more abundantly upon [them]" (v. 10).

18. See Jeffrey R. Holland, "Prepare to Have a Spiritual Experience When Partaking of the Sacrament," in *Excerpts from General Conference Leadership Training, April 2015;* video available from stake presidents.

19. Neil L. Andersen, "Witnessing to Live the Commandments," in *Excerpts.*

20. As Elder Robert D. Hales recently observed: "I sometimes wonder if we realize in this covenant that we're taking that we are witnessing to the Father, . . . bearing testimony to the Father" ("Always Remember Him," in *Excerpts*).

Covenant Keepers and the Family of God
Camille Fronk Olson

1. Naomi W. Randall, "I Am a Child of God," *Hymns of The Church of Jesus Christ of Latter-day Saints* (Salt Lake City: The Church of Jesus Christ of Latter-day Saints, 1985), no. 301.
2. Young Women theme, available at https://www.lds.org/young-women/personal-progress/young-women-theme?lang=eng.
3. Joseph F. Smith, *Joseph F. Smith* [manual], in Teachings of Presidents of the Church series (Salt Lake City: The Church of Jesus Christ of Latter-day Saints, 1998), 100.

Women of Dedication, Faith, Determination, and Action
M. Russell Ballard

1. George Gendron, "The Talk of the Inc. 500," *Inc.*, 1 September 1991; available at http://www.inc.com/magazine/19910901/4813.html.
2. Wallace Stegner, *The Gathering of Zion: The Story of the Mormon Trail* (New York: McGraw-Hill, 1964), 13.
3. *Daughters in My Kingdom: The History and Work of Relief Society* (Salt Lake City: The Church of Jesus Christ of Latter-day Saints, 2011), 14–15.
4. *The Early Show*, CBS, 19 December 2000; as quoted in Jane Clayson Johnson, *I Am a Mother* (Salt Lake City: Deseret Book, 2007), 51.
5. Julie B. Beck, "'And upon the Handmaids in Those Days Will I Pour Out My Spirit,'" *Ensign*, May 2010, 11.
6. See Andrew Keen, *The Cult of the Amateur: How Today's Internet Is Killing Our Culture* (New York: Crown Business, 2007).
7. Harold B. Lee, *Stand Ye in Holy Places* (Salt Lake City: Deseret Book, 1974), 309.
8. L. Tom Perry, "The Church: Scaffolding for Our Lives," Brigham Young University–Idaho devotional, 24 January 2012; available at http://www2.byui.edu/Presentations/Transcripts/Devotionals/2012_01_24_Perry.htm.
9. Dallin H. Oaks, "Same-Gender Attraction," *Ensign*, October 1995, 7.
10. Oaks, "Apostasy and Restoration," *Ensign*, May 1995, 87.

11. Joseph Smith, *History of The Church of Jesus Christ of Latter-day Saints,* 7 vols., edited by B. H. Roberts (Salt Lake City: The Church of Jesus Christ of Latter-day Saints, 1932–51), 3:30; from an editorial published in *Elders' Journal,* July 1838, 44.

12. M. Russell Ballard, "Stay in the Boat and Hold On!" *Ensign,* November 2014, 89–92.

13. Smith, *History of the Church,* 5:25; from a discourse given by Joseph Smith on 9 June 1842 in Nauvoo, Illinois; reported by Eliza R. Snow.

14. Ballard, "Women of Righteousness," *Ensign,* April 2002, 70.

15. Jane Carter Robinson Hindly, "Jane C. Robinson Hindly Reminiscences and Diary," Church History Library.

Contributors

ELDER M. RUSSELL BALLARD is a member of the Quorum of the Twelve Apostles of The Church of Jesus Christ of Latter-day Saints. He has been serving as an Apostle since 6 October 1985.

He was born in 1928 in Salt Lake City, Utah, and as a young man, attended the University of Utah and served a mission to England. In 1974, he was called as president of the Canada Toronto Mission where he was serving when called to the First Quorum of the Seventy in April of 1976. He later served as a member of the Presidency of the Seventy from February 1980 to October 1985.

Prior to his call as a full-time Church leader, Elder Ballard had interests in automotive, real estate, and investment businesses. He has served on many Church and civic committees and boards.

He married Barbara Bowen in the Salt Lake Temple in 1951. They are the parents of two sons and five daughters.

TAD R. CALLISTER and KATHRYN LOUISE CALLISTER have been married since 1968. They have taught early-morning seminary together and served in the Canada Toronto Mission as mission president and wife. Sister Callister currently serves as the Activity Days leader and Brother Callister serves as Sunday School general president. They love spending time with their six children and twenty-nine grandchildren.

MARY KATHLEEN EYRING and her husband, Jacob Carter, live in Utah. They both teach at Brigham Young University.

LAUREL CHRISTENSEN DAY, a runner, a Jane Austen devotee, and a sought-after speaker, grew up in California, Kentucky, and Missouri. After serving in the California Riverside Mission, she went on to earn a bachelor's degree from Brigham Young University and later received a master's degree. She has spent most of her career at Deseret Book Company, where she is currently Vice President of Product Development.

FIONA GIVENS WAS born in Nairobi and educated in Catholic convent schools. While studying in Frankfurt-am-Main she converted to The Church of Jesus Christ of Latter-day Saints. She has degrees in French and German from the University of Richmond where she also obtained a master's degree in European history. She is coauthor with her husband, Terryl, of *The God Who Weeps* and *Crucible of Doubt*. She and Terryl are the proud parents of six remarkable children and the grandparents of five fonts of fun. They currently reside in Montpelier, Virginia.

Prior to her marriage to President Russell M. Nelson in April 2006, WENDY WATSON NELSON was a professor of marriage and family therapy for twenty-five years, the last thirteen at Brigham Young University. She holds a PhD in family therapy and gerontology.

Sister Nelson has served as stake Relief Society president, stake Primary president, and was the chair of the BYU Women's Conference in 1999 and 2000.

She was born in Raymond, Alberta, Canada, to Leonard David and Laura Byrde McLean Watson.

CAMILLE FRONK OLSON is a professor of Ancient Scripture at Brigham Young University and chair of the department of Ancient Scripture. She has researched and published often on women in scripture and LDS doctrine. She is a former member of the Young Women general board and served a mission to Toulouse, France. She loves taking long walks through the natural beauty of God's creations and sticking her hands in dirt, which she calls "gardening." When she married Paul Olson, she scored by also inheriting a son and a daughter and now four delightful grandchildren.

Bonnie L. Oscarson and her husband, Paul, served as mission president and wife in the Sweden Göteborg Mission and thirty-three years later returned to Sweden to serve as temple president and matron in the Stockholm Sweden Temple. They are the parents of seven children and have twenty-eight grandchildren, all of whom are budding geniuses. Forty-one years passed between the time she started as a student at Brigham Young University and her graduation, but she got a lot of good things done during that time. She is currently serving as the Young Women general president for the Church.

Kevin and Peggy Worthen began serving as President and First Lady of Brigham Young University in 2014. They were both raised in Price, Utah, and both are BYU graduates, he in political science and law, she in English. They began dating shortly after Kevin returned from his mission in Monterrey, Mexico, while they were students at the College of Eastern Utah (now USU–Eastern). They have been married thirty-six years and are the parents of three children and have three grandchildren.

Index